THE AGE OF ENGAGE

THE AGE OF ENGAGE

Reinventing Marketing for Today's
Connected, Collaborative, and
Hyperinteractive Culture

Denise Shiffman

Hunt Street

Published by Hunt Street Press
27762 Antonio Parkway, Suite L1485
Ladera Ranch, CA 92694
info@huntstreetpress.com

Distributed by Greenleaf Book Group LP

For ordering information or special discounts for bulk purchases, please contact Greenleaf Book Group LP at 4425 Mo Pac South, Suite 600, Longhorn Building, 3rd Floor, Austin, TX 78735, (512) 891-6100.

Design and composition by Greenleaf Book Group LP
Cover design by Greenleaf Book Group LP

Publisher's Cataloging-In-Publication Data

Shiffman, Denise.
   The age of engage : reinventing marketing for today's connected, collaborative, and hyperinteractive culture / Denise Shiffman. -- 1st ed.
      p. cm.
   Includes bibliographical references and index.
   LCCN 2007935317
   ISBN-13: 978-0-9798028-0-5
   ISBN-10: 0-9798028-0-6

   1. Internet marketing. 2. Marketing-Technological innovations.
   3. Interactive marketing.   I. Title.

HF5415.1265.S55 2007   658.8'72028546
                            QBI07-600233

Printed in the United States of America on acid-free paper

12 11 10 09 08 07   10 9 8 7 6 5 4 3 2 1

First Edition

to evan,
a gift beyond my wildest imagination

CONTENTS

FOREWORD

There are thousands of books on marketing. Most extol the need to focus on customers; be customer centric, create great experiences, promote and defend your brand. Marketing is said to be done primarily through traditional media—print and broadcast which are one-way, static, and centralized. Public relations is the business of communicating and controlling "messages." Customer input is achieved through solicitation—as in surveys and focus groups. Customers are outside the boundaries of the firm and not really engaged in actual innovation, let alone ongoing product and service co-creation. All this is best summed up in the famous "Four Ps" of marketing—having the right *product*, being in the right *place* with the optimal *price* and effective (one way) *promotion*.

Call it Marketing 1.0.

For many years I and others have talked about some important drivers that require a complete rethinking of marketing.

Technology

The first is the new Web or Web 2.0. As Anthony Williams and I explain in *Wikinomics*, there are many names for this new Web: Web 2.0, the living Web, the Hypernet, the active Web, the read/write Web. Call it what you like—the sentiment is the same. We're on to something big. We are all participating in the rise of a global, ubiquitous platform for computation and collaboration that is reshaping nearly every aspect of human affairs.

The old Web was about Web sites, clicks, and "eyeballs." In some ways it resembled the old broadcast media more than today's new collaborative Web. As users and computing power multiply, and easy-to-use tools proliferate, the Internet is evolving into a global, living, networked computer that anyone can program, whether building a business on Amazon.com, producing a video clip for YouTube, creating a community around a Flickr photo collection, or editing the astronomy entry on Wikipedia.

This new Web already links more than a billion people directly and (unlike Web 1.0) is reaching out to the physical world, connecting countless inert objects from hotel doors to cars. It is beginning to deliver dynamic new services—from free long distance video telephony to remote brain surgery. It covers the planet like a skin.

The New Generation of Consumers—The Net Generation

The second driver is the arrival of the Net Generation—the offspring of the baby boomers. This is the first generation to grow up immersed in digital technologies. Born between 1977 and 1996 inclusive, this generation is bigger than the baby boom itself, and through sheer demographic muscle they will dominate the 21st century. While it is smaller in some countries (particularly those in Western Europe), internationally, the Net generation is huge—numbering over 2 billion people. This is the first generation to grow up in the digital age and that makes them a force for collaboration. They are growing up bathed in bits. The vast majority of North American adolescents know how to use a computer, and almost ninety percent of teenagers in America say they use the

Net. The same is true in a growing number of countries around the world. Indeed, there are more youngsters in this age group who use the Net in China, than there are in the United States.

This generation is transforming marketing for many reasons, foremost being, unlike their parents in the U.S., who watched twenty-four hours of television per week, these youngsters are growing up interacting. Rather than being passive recipients of mass consumer culture, the Net Gen spend time searching, reading, scrutinizing, authenticating, collaborating, and organizing (everything from their MP3 files to protest demonstrations).

And New Paradigm's research indicates that close to half of the TV they watch they time shift—eliminating the advertisements. The old saw "half my ads work—I just don't know which half" needs revision. Marketers can be sure the half audiences never see don't work.

Economics

Because the new Web radically drops collaboration costs, the 20th century vertically integrated corporation is giving way to focused firms working within business webs. As costs continue to drop and capability continues to grow through social networks, blogs, wikis, and other tools it is now possible to view customers and consumers as part of a firm's B-web rather than being outsiders. Further, consumers can co-innovate value becoming "prosumers." Peers outside corporate boundaries, using the principles of wikinomics, can collaborate, sometimes on an astronomical scale to create goods and services—everything from encyclopedias and software to motorcycles. Social networking is becoming social production. The Web is becoming a new mode of creation.

Further transparency as a new force in the economy is shifting power towards customers. This is far more than the obligation to disclose basic financial information. Customers are gaining unprecedented access to all sorts of information about corporate behavior, operations, and performance. Armed with new tools to find information about matters that affect their interests, stakeholders now scrutinize the firm as never before. The corporation is becoming naked. Corporations have no choice but to rethink their values and behaviors—to integrate corporate citizenship into their DNA. If you're going to be naked, you'd better be buff!

As a result, customer centricity is being turned upside down. Rather than simply listening to customers, companies must and can truly *engage* them. Customers become value creators themselves through new forms of collaboration. Companies can use the Web to build rich experiences that endure. The brand, rather than being just an image, promise, or "word in the mind" as it's called, can become, in part, an actual relationship between a company and its customers.

Marketing 2.0

This completely changes marketing. The old paradigm was one of control, simple and unidirectional: firms market to customers. We create products and define their features and benefits, set prices, select places to sell products and services, and promote aggressively through advertising, public relations, direct mail, and other in-your-face programs. We control the message. B-webs transform all of these activities.

Products

Today they are mass-customized, service-intensive, and infused with the knowledge and the individual tastes of customers. Companies must constantly innovate, and product life cycles collapse. Customers now participate in creating products and services through B-webs. Products are becoming experiences. The old industrial approaches to product definition and product marketing are dying.

Price

Enabled by online marketplaces, dynamic markets and dynamic pricing are challenging vendor fixed pricing. In these early days of new price discovery mechanisms we question even the concept of a "price" as customers gain access to mechanisms that allow them to state what they're willing to pay and for what. As John Svoikla pointed out in *Red Herring* years ago, price is a crude measure. It reflects in a single number all the attributes that customers may value in a product—time, effort, craftsmanship, innovation, fashion, status, rarity, long-term value, and so on. Customers will offer various prices for products depending on conditions specified. If you deliver this afternoon I'll pay *A*. If I can buy this quantity I'll pay *B*. I'll accept certain defects and pay *C*. If someone else will pay *D*, then I'll pay *E*. Buyers and sellers exchange more information and pricing becomes fluid. Markets, not firms, will "price" products and services. New companies like Exchange Solutions now create markets where price and money are only one of the variables in value.

Place

Every B-web competes in two worlds: a physical world (marketplace) and a digital world of information (marketspace). B-webs enable firms to focus on the marketspace by creating not a great Web site but a great B-web and relationship capital. Hearts, not eyeballs, count. Within a decade, the majority of products and services in many developed countries will be sold in the market*space*.

Promotion

Advertising, promotion, publicity, public relations, and most other aspects of corporate communications are archaic concepts. They exploited unidirectional, one-to-many and one-size-fits-all media to communicate "messages" to faceless, powerless customers. The Net Generation's "N-Fluence" networks are powerful new forces that marketers must engage. Even traditional broadcast advertising can be transformed, as was the case of the Doritos Super Bowl ad contest—where Doritos engaged their customers in creating product ads (by my reckoning to great success).

The B-web and wikinomics upends control. Friction breaks among customers and between you and your customers. They often have access to near perfect information about products, and power shifts towards them. Customers, no longer external entities, participate in your firm's B-web through multidirectional, one-to-one, and highly tailored communications media. They control the marketing mix, not you. They choose the medium and the message. Rather than receiving broadcast images, they do the casting. Rather than getting messages from earnest PR professionals, they create "public opinion" online with one another.

I remember with amusement all the prognostications that the Web pioneers including Amazon, eBay, and Google were doomed to disaster because their competition was only a click away. What the doomsayers didn't understand was the power of relationships. When firms use the Web to truly engage customers, the relationships can be strong and lasting. I'm tempted to describe this as a new form of wealth, say relationship capital, which firms need to develop and manage like other forms of capital.

Go back to the pioneers; a simple, prosaic comparison between a physical bookstore and Amazon.com is instructive. A customer buys a book from an online bookstore. She can request all books on a certain topic, or author. She can indicate authors she likes and find out what other authors are enjoyed by customers who share her views. She can request a bestseller list in a category or ask for a book's daily sales status. She can ask for similar books on the same topic. Some neighborhood boutique stores deliver a few such value-added services, but many such stores have disappeared. The costs are too great relative to the revenue received.

In the physical world, these costs hinder personalized service and relationship creation. But in the interactive world, you can get to know your customer, educate her, inform her proactively, and deliver value-added services on a personal basis. You can engage in ways that are simply not possible otherwise—you can have a relationship.

The astute online bookstore e-mails her when a new book fits her personal profile. The relationship is mutual—she creates value for the seller and for other participants by contributing her views. She establishes her personal profile (makes a relationship investment) that includes registering gifts she would like to receive. She complains about something and receives a personal note within an hour, telling her how the problem has been fixed. She and the vendor develop a relationship.

Both invest by exchanging customized information and knowledge. The more she invests time and effort, the more personal the bookstore becomes. She builds loyalty to this company, not just because of the services it provides, but also because of the effort required to re-educate another company about her. For both buyer and seller, this networked relationship constitutes capital. Astute companies extract as much value—return—from the relationships as possible.

In the digital economy, the wealth embedded in customer relationships is now more important than the capital contained in land, plant, buildings, and even big bank accounts. Relationships are now assets. This "relationship capital" accumulates and provides a new foundation for marketing and sales revenue. A firm's ability to engage customers, suppliers, and other partners in mutually beneficial value exchanges determines its relationship capital.

The customer-facing aspects of relationship capital cause a profound rethinking of marketing. For the first time, companies can forge two-way, interactive, personalized relationships with all customers on a mass scale.

While the virtue of deep relationships was always self-evident in theory, in reality it wasn't practical. But now the ubiquitous, cheap, and interactive Net coupled with enormous low-cost databases enables producers to develop a meaningful direct relationship with each customer. Customers expect you to tailor each iteration of your product to their needs and wants. Sellers and buyers create an ongoing dialogue.

The Age of Engage

Denise Shiffman had done a great service by writing *The Age of Engage*. This is the first comprehensive attempt that I am aware of to present an alternative to the "Four Ps," and in doing so to define Marketing 2.0. I believe this book will be helpful for almost anyone involved in any facet of marketing. Read, apply, and prosper.

—Don Tapscott
© 2007 New Paradigm

Don Tapscott is chief executive of New Paradigm—a firm that specializes in business model innovation. He is co-author (with Anthony D. Williams) of the international bestseller *Wikinomics: How Mass Collaboration Changes Everything* and ten other business books. You can find Don at www.newparadigm.com.

ACKNOWLEDGMENTS

There are so many people to thank who directly or indirectly helped with the manuscript. Although the book didn't require primary research, there were endless hours spent tracking and researching through blogs, business books, online business publications and newspapers, and through traditional print publications. Information was gleaned from speakers at marketing tradeshows and conferences, and through one-on-one interviews. Some parts of the manuscript rely on my twenty-three years of experience in marketing and executive management, as well as my experiences at Sun Microsystems and other companies.

Several executives provided me with insight to their business and marketplace. These include Daniel Stein (EVB), Ben Elowitz (Wetpaint), Ivan Braiker (Hipcricket), Jeff Liebl (eBureau), Michael Rubenstein (Doubleclick), Scott Spencer (Doubleclick), Robert Riopelle (LiveHive Systems), Skip Brand (JiWire), and Esteban Sardera (Pairup). Others were speakers or panel participants at conferences, and they include Jason McDonell (Frito-Lay), Finlay Robb (Lego Direct 2 Consumer), Patrice Varni (Levi Strauss & Co.), Mel Clements (The Coca-Cola Company), Andrew Shih (Proctor & Gamble), Andrew Markowitz (Kraft Foods), Ken Loh (Oakley), Jamie Byrne (YouTube), Benjamin Palmer (The Barbarian Group), Sean Carver (Microsoft), Nick Grouf

(Spot Runner), David Scacco (Google), Shawn Gold (MySpace), and Cynthia Francis (Realitydigital).

My heartfelt thanks goes to Amanda West, whose continued support and encouragement got me through this process, and for being willing to read the earliest drafts. I'd also like to thank Tracey Stout for engaging in provocative philosophical discussions. Elizabeth Zack with BookCrafters, LLC provided editorial input, tightened up the manuscript, and ensured the consistency a project like this requires.

There were countless people on my blog who by commenting on articles gave me insight and a new way of thinking about some of these subjects. In addition several of the people I've worked with throughout my career both colleagues and clients have affected my thinking and philosophies on marketing. They include Ed Zander, John Loiacono, and Anil Gadre.

I can't thank enough the following people who made it possible for me to tackle this huge project; Laurie Stephan, Deborah Drisdale, David Fickes, Shannon McGuire, Natalie Simmons, Heidi Howard, Hannah Howard, Mel & Pearl, Karen & Bill, and Scott & Kim.

Finally, I'd like to thank my son Evan who inspired me to embark on a new career, stay forever young, and get a clue about almost everything.

1 | Made to Engage

STOP LISTENING TO YOUR CUSTOMERS AND START
INTERACTING WITH THEM.

For years you've been told to talk to your customers, listen to your customers, get their input, and hear their frustrations. So, you run focus groups and send out surveys. You invite customers to your offices for a sit-down. The problem is that, as business people with conflicting agendas, we don't actually listen very well. And customers still feel they aren't being heard. Worse, customers can only tell us their response to our product or a problem. They can't dream for us, or help us break through with an innovative or creative concept.

Or can they?

Over the past ten years, the evolution of the Internet, including the most recent Web 2.0 technologies, has had a dramatic impact on marketplace behavior. Web 2.0, which I'll explain in a moment, has driven a change in our culture unleashing an environment where customers and prospects are ready and willing (even demanding!) to get deeply involved with our brand, products, and services. But now their involvement includes using our brand and our content in ways we didn't intend, and hacking our product, or blending it with another product (called *mashing*), thereby treating the warranty with reckless abandon.

Another challenge marketers contend with is customers who have the ability to voice their opinion to millions on blogs or podcasts, or on Web sites designed to give them a voice. As a response to this evolving consumer influence, many executives and marketers have chosen to hunker down, protect their brands and intellectual property, and remain in a state of command and control. That is a mistake, and risks the tremendous opportunity made possible by the evolving Web.

The technology, functions, and features of this new Web create a significant change from the original, static Web *(Web 1.0)*. Web 2.0 is jet propulsion for the 21st century. The invention of jet propulsion made the world a smaller place by connecting vast numbers of people. It sped our ability to make and sell products and mobilized cultural change (not to mention helped win a war and rocketed man to the moon). This new Web is proving to have the same effect (well, maybe not on space travel, yet). The technology itself is interesting, but it's what people are choosing to do with it that has altered the way we do business. It has also created a cultural shift from the insular read-learn-follow-along consumer behavior to the participative, collaborative, user-generated, sharing, social, global, open, interactive generation. This is the age of engage.

The Web is fast becoming the real-time information center for all human knowledge and behavior, what many call *Web 3.0*. It's more than the books, movies, and music now digitized and available on the Web. We have created this knowledge center by searching, purchasing, linking, and tagging. Every day we leave our fingerprint of thoughts, needs, wants, and behaviors. Tapping into this information will forever change marketing. It doesn't matter if you sell to business or to consumers. If you haven't quite put your arms around the social Web technologies and incorporated them deeply into your product definition and marketing strategy, read on. I have some ideas that may help.

The Rules of Engagement

There are so many terms used in the lexicon of the Web, they can make writing about it rather confusing. Web 2.0, a term coined by an executive at O'Reilly Media, refers to many of the social and live aspects of the Web including blogging, podcasting, tagging, social sites, Ajax, RSS, and a few other technologies, functions, and services.[1] The new technologies coming out in *Web 3.0*, a term that first appeared in *The New York Times* in 2006, create a Web that offers meaning—where the sum of all knowledge and online behavior can be accessed.[2] The descriptor I like best is used by Doc Searls, a well-known industry pundit, and one of the authors of *The Cluetrain Manifesto* as well as editor of the *Linux Journal*. He created the title *Live Web* to describe the dramatic change from the static Web of the 1990s to today's interactive Web.[3]

I agree with Doc Searls: We need to think of the Web as alive, as an ecosystem with a heartbeat that is constantly moving and changing in order to create engaging, interactive marketing, and valuable business interactions at each touchpoint. The result for marketers is the ability to create, influence, and participate in the conversations that make up markets. So, for the purposes of this book, I am opting to use *Live Web* as the all-encompassing term for Web 2.0 and Web 3.0 and everything in between.

The Live Web is a place where people meet, converse, create, and learn. With all of these interactions, it is fast becoming a vast human brain trust—a repository we can search, analyze, and organize to better engage the world around us. This evolution of the Web has turned marketing on its head. The Live Web has established users who generate their own content to express themselves or their ideas about your products, and the passionate few who open up proprietary products to add to or change them. It isn't a conspiracy to hijack your brands, but it can make your job more difficult, and it should compel companies to rethink and reinvent their relationship with prospects, customers, and partners.

Today's hacking, mashing, and public expression is a natural evolution of technology catching up with human behavior. Without a doubt, hackers are a part of American culture. For the past several decades, the marketplace has changed products to fit personal needs or tastes.

DJs scratched vinyl to change the sound of a song, or teenage girls mixed nail polish to invent their own color, or they cut the legs off their jeans to make shorts. All of these product hacks were ingrained into our culture and later became a part of the mainstream. So, it's not surprising we would see this behavior on the Web.

We're in the midst of great change, and it's this change from the static, flat, corporate-created Web to the interactive, social, user-created Web that has accelerated consumer influence. And this is just the beginning. We've seen a broad spectrum of reaction to this creative consumer behavior. There are companies that believe their brands *are* being hijacked. They fight their own customers, and they use the legal system to assert control over the matter. Other companies are hopping in blindly with both feet, trying to feel their way through the change. Without much of a strategy, they encourage interactive customer behavior but aren't sure what the marketing impact will be. Finally, there are companies designed around engaging, interactive behavior. They encourage and take advantage of the new dynamic consumer interactions bring to their products, and are inspired by them. And throughout this book, we will see what happens to companies which execute on these differing paths.

The rules to the marketplace have changed. Audiences demand openness and transparency. Where once we could define and build a product, launch it, and wait for customer orders, today we must engage the marketplace early and continue to interact with audiences in real-time. From product definition to development, from positioning to advertising, and most certainly from sales to customer service, any function or all can be open to and integrate customer and partner interactivity. The Live Web makes it much easier to create real-time community around your product or service. Engaging your audiences will give you the keys to success.

Marketing Reinvented

The original, static Web drew millions of companies online to offer information about their products, and to sell their wares. The second coming of the Web has transformed the online marketplace into an interactive, personal, and communal space. Consumers have been transformed from passive viewers and choosers to active and powerful beacons collectively creating winners and losers. Breaking through the clutter of voices in this new marketplace is an audacious challenge for any marketer. E-mail, viral, search, social, widgets, avatars, authenticity, and story make up the new language. New media, tools, and technologies have to be mastered to remain in the game. In this reinvention of marketing, it is the fast, the unique, the innovative and creative, the socially connected, and most importantly, those who engage their audience that will win.

Nowhere has the effects of the Live Web had a greater impact than on advertising. The Live Web has rewritten the fundamentals of the advertising industry's conventional media vehicles: television and news and magazine publishing. These industries have lost their cachet and are continually losing their ability to draw big audiences. Eyeballs have moved to the Internet, to mobile phones, and to game consoles. Consumer wallets are following close behind. The change wouldn't be so gut-wrenching had the entertainment and publishing industries jumped on the online bandwagon quickly and whole-heartedly. They could have transformed their business models and led the revolution. They were warned.

Instead, we have had a massive audience shift from prime time to anytime, disaggregating broadcast programming from its advertising revenue stream. Profitability is being driven out of the newspaper business as millions of customers move their news consumption online to news aggregation and social sites, including Digg, Techmeme, or The Huffington Post. For where eyeballs go, ad dollars follow. Worse, classified ads—the revenue stream newspapers have always been able to rely on—have moved online to Craigslist, Google, Yahoo!, and eBay. Content creation is up for grabs, content delivery is moving to new, untried media, and the traditional content owners have one heck of a challenge getting back in the game.

Both magazine and newspaper publishers are caught in the painful Catch-22 of driving their audience online away from traditional formats while hoping that Web ad revenues will grow fast enough to make up for the losses they're experiencing in print. And it isn't happening.[4, 5] News Corp.'s Times Newspapers Ltd. lost approximately $90 million in 2005.[6] London's *The Guardian* and *The Observer* newspapers lost $35 million in 2005. McClatchy Company, the second-largest U.S. newspaper by circulation, announced a fiscal year 2006 fourth-quarter loss of almost $280 million.[7]

In 2006 we started to see some big steps forward from some traditional publications. *USA Today* offers its online content free, and has developed an interactive and social news site that enables readers to comment and write reviews, upload photos, and create their own blog. On the front page, blogs from editors as well as readers are featured. *The Wall Street Journal* online has added most popular article voting, and the ability to create a personalized view of the publication. They also include staff writers' email addresses at the end of each article, enabling unprecedented access. *The New York Times* online enables readers to share articles and to comment. They also publish a number of blogs, offering a more personal relationship with staff writers and columnists. Although all of these functions now seem obvious, they are ground-breaking for what were highly insular organizations.

Figuring out how to collaborate to expand their business models has been more difficult, however. Several news publishers have come to the realization that it is better to dance with the enemy, and they are now making deals to sell classified ads through the major search sites. But for all of this change, they still have not figured out how to revive their kingpin status. News has been usurped by the masses. Soldiers and civilians blog the details and emotions of a war. Passers-by catch a catastrophic event on their mobile phone camera or digicam. Bloggers instantly talk, link, and display what is happening. News sites like CNN, which encourages visitors to upload their photos or videos, are eclipsed by Flickr's mass of event-tagged photos.[8] Professional journalists get the hard facts, but it's getting harder and harder to monetize their content. The traditional media industry doesn't need to catch up; they need to reinvent themselves.

Where we get our entertainment and consume ads has shifted to the online elite: Google's YouTube, News Corp.'s MySpace, and Yahoo!. And even they will need to innovate to continue to charm audiences. Entertainment is shifting, disaggregating, and re-aggregating in new ways. Major consumer brands including Pepsi (PepsiStuff.com), Nike (Joga.com), and Anheuser-Busch (Bud.tv) have set up their own Web entertainment and social sites. Brightcove and PermissionTV offer hosting services that make this simple for anyone to do. But to pull in big audiences, you may spend as much as $30 million to kick off your own entertainment Web site. If that's not an option, companies can partner with Web TV companies including blip.tv, SuperDeluxe, and Veoh which are focused on user-generated programming, Network2 which aggregates Web TV programming from dozens of sources, and Joost which runs only copyrighted, professional programming. The Live Web has obliterated the traditional media plan and ad buy. Where to place ads isn't just about reach or target audience anymore, it's about audience interaction.

This sweeping change across the media landscape has given marketing a fresh start. The fundamental strategies companies use to develop and differentiate their products, and then communicate their value to the marketplace, have been greatly altered. The Live Web has enabled users to create community and share information, ideas, and, well, entertainment on a scale never before possible. We are now marketing in the consumer-powered age. This is Marketing 2.0.

User-generated content as seen on YouTube and MySpace—as well as on hundreds of other sites—is drawing millions of consumers further from their television sets. A daily dose of 100 million video streams are served and seventy-thousand new video clips uploaded on YouTube alone.[9] Over 26 million visitors access the social networking site Facebook each month.[10] Blogs, podcasts, and personal videos are developed by anyone on any subject and can draw audiences in the millions. No longer can marketers push their message onto an audience. Consumers and business purchasers now have the ability to choose whom they will listen to and when. The power in the marketing relationship with the customer has shifted. Advertisers must be invited into our homes, and onto our computers, iPods, and mobile phones.

It's this permission by the consumer or business person which Seth Godin writes about in his book, *Permission Marketing: Turning Strangers into Friends and Friends into Customers*. Permission is fundamental to marketing going forward. The most astounding result of permission marketing is that almost all of the power has moved to the purchaser. Not only do they choose whether or not to listen to your message, with just a click of a few keys and several minutes of their time, they can find out what customers think, the price of competitive products, and if you manufacture in a country that abuses child labor laws.

The implementation of marketing in the age of engage has been dubbed *Marketing 2.0*, as this essential business discipline has leaped to a new level on the marketing continuum.[11] In the 1960s and 1970s we focused on marketing to the masses. The rise of broadcast television as a medium to sell products created huge brands. There was less competition, and consumers learned to trust marketers. This was marketing at ground zero—*Marketing 0.0*.

By the 1980s we could see the flaws in mass marketing, the dollars wasted in chasing people who weren't interested in the message. Segmenting, targeting, and niche marketing became the cattle call throughout the 1980s and 1990s. In this timeframe, the "Four Ps" marketing paradigm had taken hold. The creation of marketing as a strategic business process, including product, price, place, and promotion, defined *Marketing 1.0*. Companies focused their marketing budget on programs that targeted specific audiences, and that created better marketing. For most companies, segmenting made sense since the cost to create the mass brand through mass advertising and promotions, the way Coke and Pepsi have done, was and still is too high. Today, it clearly makes no sense for companies to blow their *entire* marketing budget on Super Bowl ads (although, amazingly, companies still do just that).

Marketing 2.0 offers a compelling new paradigm for how to implement interactive and engaging marketing that simultaneously targets individuals and the mass market. Amazon does this quite well. Based on what terms you've searched or what you've previously purchased on Amazon, the site offers suggestions for what you might want to purchase in the future. Such behavioral targeting can be implemented by any company or ad network. Every time users type words into a search box (Google, Yahoo!, MSN, or other), they give the search engine information about their behavior, needs, and desires. All of those bits put together make it simple to target specific ads to a person's needs at exactly the right time. We are now in the era of marketing to the individual, and doing it on a broad scale.

Increased audience information and interactivity has raised the creativity bar and driven inventiveness into marketing. CareerBuilder.com took a simple, yet highly creative email concept sent only to eighteen-hundred employees of the company and its ad agency, and turned it into a huge, viral marketing weapon eventually reaching over 60 million people. JetBlue posted an apology on YouTube for its poor treatment of customers over a snowed-in President's Day weekend.[12] In four days, the company reached two-hundred-thousand interested viewers at no cost, and the video was reposted on countless blogs.

Smart marketers are going to find the age of engage a good time to be in marketing. True, there is more complexity and less control. Yet the authentic, on-target, timely message will enable successful products on a broader scale than in the past. Taking advantage of the efficiencies of the Web, more products will have the opportunity to attract consumers, or easily be found by them. Products that meet a real market need, offered by even the smallest companies, can find an audience, and experience exceptional growth through top-of-page organic search results or through word-of-mouth. The Live Web offers small companies an advantage previously found only in large companies, the ability to collaborate with strangers, customers, and partners no matter where they may be located.

With more competitors, alternatives, and confusing marketing messages pushed out to the masses, the goal is to take advantage of the Live Web to break through the noise. To do that you need to understand what has changed, what is new, and how to take advantage of the right tools and vehicles to achieve success with your product. Marketing 2.0 isn't just about moving your advertising online. It is about incorporating podcasts, blogs, wikis, RSS, user-generated content, social sites, and much more into your strategy. It is also about building products integrated with social elements, affiliate elements, open interfaces, and sharing capabilities. These are the components that engage. The Live Web has enabled and driven these activities, and pushes us to manage our brands in new ways. By being open, authentic, public, and porous, we can begin to take advantage of the collective force that is now the Web.

More than ever before, marketing fundamentals will need to be solid. It's not new technology alone that drives a successful product, it is the unique value offered, the well-targeted audience (or person), the clear, consistent message, and the right mix of media to deliver the message. The magic of great marketing creative (those funny or provocative ads and emails), and the potency of meeting a specific need in the market are still key drivers to product adoption. However, how you reach your audience, deliver your product, and develop customer loyalty will never be the same.

The Live Web provides a key advantage to marketers. It is quick and easy to evaluate and measure results of an online marketing campaign whether the vehicle used is paid search, email marketing, or PR. Online tools enable even the smallest business to evaluate the success of each marketing activity. This level of accountability should get your attention. Marketing budgets generally receive a great deal of scrutiny. Good metrics that prove out the benefits of marketing to the brand and the bottom line are essential. Marketing accountability will get more attention in this new age.

Yet, the revived marketing landscape is far from perfect. Click fraud, spam, and *phishing* (fake email or Web sites designed to lure users into providing their personal or financial information) are common today and appear to be getting worse. Further, the theft or accidental release of corporate-owned private user data has happened all too many times. When AOL accidentally released the *click path* (online search behavior) of over six-hundred-and-fifty-thousand subscribers, a collective shudder went through the marketing community, and alarms went off with privacy advocates.[13] Marketers will get so much better at their jobs if they can analyze and use information collected from consumers. But privacy concerns are tantamount and each breach makes everyone look bad. The technical community and businesses have a great deal invested in fixing these problems and work in that direction has started.

Marketers are still learning the ropes. Wal-Mart, McDonald's, and Wendy's all broke their trust with consumers when they produced online ads or fake blogs (known as *flogs*) designed to look like they came from consumers.[14] A lie won't stay a secret for long in this consumer-powered Web. Ads, blogs, or other marketing tools not identified as such, and meant to fool, trick, or deceive consumers will be shunned (along with the advertiser). Authenticity and trust are more important now that anyone can communicate the truth to millions. Advertisers need to be worried less about the FCC and more about the blogger sitting at his home computer. According to Don Tapscott and David Ticoll in their book, *The Naked Corporation*, "Transparency is being done to the firm whether it likes it or not." Companies that are open, authentic, and actively transparent reinforce their values and priorities with their audiences.

The Live Web drives us to reinvent our organizational behavior, our product development process and design, our partnerships, and of course, our marketing. This book will crystallize how the Live Web has marshaled change within the vast discipline of marketing and across the company. In response to the shake-up among traditional marketing vehicles (television, newspapers, and magazines) and in an effort to take advantage of the online marketplace, more than a dozen new marketing vehicles have been invented, forcing marketers to rethink their strategies designed to attract customers to their products. It is in our understanding of how the ground has shifted and our ability to adjust our perspective that will help us market better and stand a chance at breaking through the clutter.

The changes I see are not just about marketing tactics, they are about organizing yourself or your company to market more effectively and to engage. Building a succinct strategy to manage and drive all of these activities will help you see past the chaos.

A New Marketing Perspective

It's time to rethink what we know, and approach products and markets with a new perspective. One of the biggest drags on the ability for companies to build and market Live Web-optimized products is the organizational hierarchy and departmental silos so common today. The Live Web is about openness, sharing, collaborating, and interacting. Companies that incorporate these elements empower their organizations' ability to innovate, establish differentiation, and connect with their audiences. And although full coverage on the subject of how companies organize is too big for this book, I will touch on it in Chapter Two to illustrate how core philosophies of the Web need to become fundamental tenets of business in order to fully execute on the Live Web opportunity.

It's true, marketing has gone through dramatic change, but let's not throw out the bath with the bathwater. The most fundamental marketing concepts still hold true. There must be a unique value tied to your product if it is going to rise to the top and get noticed—but product value isn't static. We need to know how to reinvent value and ingrain that in our processes. This is the focus of Chapter Three.

As we venture into this new marketing life cycle, we take a fresh look at all aspects of a product, from how we define and develop it, to how we differentiate it, to how we communicate about it and through which media channels. We need to know and plan for the journey we intend for our customers, and how to influence the communities on the Live Web that can help or hurt the process. More than a tagline or communications platform, this consistent and inspiring voice defines a company for customers and prospects. Creating a compelling voice and story is the focus of Chapter Four.

The Web can be viral, feverish, and full of opportunities. It can also create a vicious cycle of misinformation. In just seconds, our blemishes are blasted to millions and discussed by hundreds of thousands. We are caught on video and in photos. Creating an open, authentic, and effective image takes perseverance, and the ability to reveal ourselves which goes against our comfort zone. Staying true to our core philosophy, mission, and strategy allows the *Webosphere*—the world of people that talk, interact, and live on the Web—to settle on the truth. Chapter Five provides the needed guide, and opportunities to validate your brand and ensure credibility.

All of this is about the user behavior catalyzed by the Live Web. The meeting places, communication platforms, and user-generated behavior mark the vicinity within which we are now marketing. We are seeing the democratization of marketing. We have lost absolute control over our brands. There is much to do to get some of that control back, and it won't be through lawsuits. In addition, we will be driven to treat employees with greater respect now that they have a grand platform to discuss their gripes (and they can do this fairly anonymously).

As employees ourselves, we need to manage our etrail. Managers and recruiters can and will find out about most things we've posted on the Internet if we're not careful. Further, marketers who mislead will be undone quickly by the online underground. Juicy gossip about a company's missteps makes for great viral email. Chapter Six discusses the myriad neighborhoods on the Web and the growing influence of consumer voices, and advises marketers how to navigate these sometimes-murky waters. And as marketers we need to embrace the new marketing vehicles and determine how to successfully distribute and manage our brand, image, and message which will be covered in Chapter Seven.

The Live Web gives marketers the opportunity to expand their knowledge, and increase their influence over the corporation. Now, companies are required to have a core competency in marketing just to participate in the marketplace. And this drives marketers to step up to learning the technology, actively trialing new products, and commenting and socializing online to stay fresh and inventive. In Chapter Eight, the needed perspective and tools are brought to light.

Before I go any further, it's time to elaborate on the Live Web, and the technologies, tools, services, platforms, and innovative companies that bring the potential of engagement to our fingertips.

Understanding the Live Web

This isn't your Web of just five years ago. This is a new Web, an interactive, user-generated, linking, social environment. Take a look at a simple comparison of what's changed.

Web 1.0	Web 2.0
Static	Live
Publish	Interact
Inform	Engage
Link	Tag
Sell	Socialize
Control	Collaborate

What exactly is in Web 2.0 that has brought about so much change? To start, there are functions including blogging, podcasting, tagging, and widgets, technologies such as RSS, wikis, and Ajax, and social features such as comments, personal profiles, voting, and sharing content. These features, functions, services, and technologies have spawned the live, social, user-generated culture of today's Web. Where one person or company communicated to many people on the original Web, today many people simultaneously communicate to many other people, making it simple to socialize, collaborate, and share. Following, I will elaborate on the activities that have changed the Web—and the world in which we live and work.

Weblogs, more commonly referred to as *blogs*, are so popular that a new blog is started every second of every day. Blogs enable anyone to write about anything that comes to mind. Sitting at a home computer, a mom can blog about the trials and tribulations of raising a toddler. Teenagers can blog about dating, school, or their parents. An environmental enthusiast can blog tips and ideas each of us can use to help save the environment. CEOs can blog their point of view on products, competitors, the economy, the industry they are in, or just about anything they feel like. Blogs give individuals a voice, and according to Technorati people have spoken up to the tune of 70 million blogs (as of this writing). Doc Searls writes this about blogs:

> Blogs are journals, not sites. They are written, not built…The writing is more conversational than homiletic…That means its authors are *speaking*, and not just "creating content." They speak to readers and other bloggers that speak back, through e-mails, comments or on blogs of their own. Like all forms of life, blogging remains unfinished for the duration. ([Web] Site content, on the other hand, is finished at one time, then replaced with other finished content.)[15]

It is virtually impossible to talk about blogging without mentioning the book *Naked Conversations* by Shel Israel and Robert Scoble. Getting to the heart of what makes blogging so unique and how it has established a new Web generation, the authors describe the evolution of this phenomenon and its impact on society and business.

The ability to syndicate blogs via RSS gives blogging its jet fuel. Really simple syndication (RSS) enables bloggers to syndicate their blog posts (articles), and it offers readers the ability to receive dozens or hundreds of blog posts, podcasts, or news events in real-time right on their desktop, laptop, or mobile phone. RSS readers such as Google Reader, Pluck, or Newsgator's NetNewsWire receive, organize, and distribute RSS feeds. You can even receive feeds of what's being searched the most, or what topic of conversation among bloggers is most popular on the Web at any given moment. RSS feeds help marketers keep their finger on the pulse of what's happening in the marketplace.

But for businesses, RSS does something else. It separates content (crown jewels) from its format (your Web site and brand), which drives us to manage distributed content in new ways. Copyright and control over content will help define the evolution of the Live Web. It will also define the leaders and laggards—those who participate and those who try to control. Participating in the Live Web means marketing differently by using alternative means of attracting audiences to your message and back to your blog or Web site.

Another medium for delivering content is the podcast. In the simplest terms, *podcasts* are streamable and downloadable radio or TV shows. The name comes from content originally designed for the iPod, but podcasts can be played on any music players, mobile phones, PCs, and laptops. With Apple TV, you can listen or watch podcasts on your television. Podcasts began as audio only and felt much like listening to the radio. They quickly evolved to include video, and have become mini TV shows. Many mainstream news and financial organizations, including the BBC, CNN, and *The Wall Street Journal*, offer podcasts. Authors and bloggers extend their subject expertise through a podcast.

There are podcasts on entertainment, parenting, the environment, how-to, science fiction, and outer space, among many other subjects. One of my favorites is Mignon Fogarty's *Grammar Girl's Quick and Dirty Tips for Better Writing*. The flexibility of time and place for tuning into a podcast is its engaging feature. You can listen in your car, on a train, on a plane, while waiting at the doctor's office, or in a hotel room—just about anywhere you can carry a mobile phone or music player. And if there are podcasts you like to listen to regularly, you can get the RSS feed for the podcast sent to your desktop (or any device) in real-time. Podcasts are a great format for learning and communicating.

One of the biggest impacts on business, I believe, will come from wikis. A *wiki* refers to a Web site enabled by wiki technology. Wikis enable multiple users to simultaneously edit content on a Web page in a standardized and easy-to-use format—that is, in plain *human* language. You don't have to know HTML or any other computer language. A wiki makes it audaciously simple to break down internal and external corporate walls enabling people and projects to quickly gain from the knowledge, expertise, and support of others. This technology will be the catalyst for global and universal collaboration.

The extraordinary success of the online encyclopedia, Wikipedia, with over 1.7 million articles which are continuously updated, attests to the desire people have to donate their time and energy online. In Minnesota, for example, concerned citizens collaborate on a wiki (www.map150.org) to impact public policy. Combining their ideas and setting an agenda, they have made their voices heard by the politicians and lobbyists who too often create partisanship and gridlock rather than policy. Wikis are starting to see adoption inside corporations too. Early implementations have included the use of wikis for software development, online education and training, project management, technical support, customer relationship management, and research and development.

Tagging, also known as *social bookmarking*, is another Live Web phenomenon. Del.icio.us, Technorati, and BlueDot, are just a few of the popular tagging sites. The basic idea is that instead of bookmarking a Web page that you're interested in for later reference in your browser, you can bookmark it to a Web site that helps you organize information for easy retrieval from anywhere (laptop, hotel room, mobile phone). But much more than that, it allows you to make your bookmark public, thereby adding a social or community aspect to it. You can see what people on the Web are bookmarking at any point in time, which indicates what's being viewed or talked about. Flickr, Yahoo! Photos, Webshots, Bubbleshare, and Zoomr make it simple for you to upload, tag, and share photos with the rest of the world—a conversation of images instead of words.

Most companies, regardless of size, have not yet embraced the bookmarking phenomenon. Yet, you would think by now, most companies would have incorporated bookmarking links in their Web sites, making it quick and easy for viewers to add Web page content to the public discussion, keep it for reference, or share it with friends or colleagues. Tagging can extend your brand and your message.

Interactivity is the key to capturing audience attention, time, and interest, and *Ajax*, short for Asynchronous JavaScript and XML, is a suite of technologies that make Web sites interactive. You could say, Ajax puts "live" in Live Web. Enabling updates to specific elements on a Web page (without loading the entire page), the Web development languages and scripting tools enable separate and interesting applications like news or weather feeds, chat, IM (instant messaging), blogs, or other features to be embedded right in the page. It gives Web pages the rich, responsive, and dynamic feel found in desktop software. And for companies that don't sell software or have a software interface to their product, their Web site is the user-interface to the company—the ease of interaction, intelligence, and personality. Ajax enables companies to create Web pages—and therefore, companies—that are engaging.

A by-product of Ajax is the destruction of Web site analytics which track page views and hits in order to define a Web site's success, size, and growth. These functions no longer carry much meaning since users can interact with elements of Web pages without those interactions being counted as page views. And, hundreds of objects on each page that are pulled from the server count as a hit even though a person isn't clicking on anything. If we're going to have a better understanding of the growth and success of our Web sites, or our competitor's Web sites, then Web analytics tools will need to evolve to catch up with the Live Web. (And as of this writing, Nielson and comScore are working on that.)

Widgets are the latest marketing tool to explode in popularity. *Widgets* are essentially embeddable code. Designed to look and behave like automated applets (small applications), widgets are easily grabbed from one Web site, and embedded in another. YouTube offers the prominent example with its embeddable video-player widget. Any blog or Web site can play a YouTube video on their site in the YouTube widget without installing special software or writing any software code. Even better, no matter who created the video and uploaded it to YouTube, it moves around the Web under the YouTube logo.

Social features of the Live Web are the most talked about, and have created the biggest winners in this new age: MySpace and YouTube. Tens of millions of users set up their own pages on MySpace. They upload pictures, talk about themselves or their interests, and share and link up with thousands of "friends" (often they are strangers). Social networking sites are defined by the features that enable users to publicly share photos, videos, and content they produce themselves or simply like, and then talk, IM, chat, or blog about them. Social features found on traditional corporate sites include the ability for users to share their comments or vote on a specific subject.

Millions of people are participating in the user-generated content (UGC) groundswell. Digg, Second Life, Flickr, MySpace, and YouTube epitomize the user centricity of the Live Web. Whether a news center, virtual world, photo sharing or social networking site, these environments only work if users create the content or link to the site. The more users, the more functional and interesting the site becomes. The Live Web is about more than connecting people, but enabling them to create and participate in the conversation. Marketers are learning how to embrace UGC, as well as participate in and influence the conversation consumers generate.

In 2006, the raging discussion across marketing news and blog sites was whether or not marketers should be advertising on MySpace to get access to this 100 million plus audience. Along with other big name brands, Honda Element with over thirty-eight-thousand friends, Burger King with over one-hundred-and-thirty-thousand friends, and Paris Hilton who has over one-hundred-and-fifty-thousand friends have set up pages on MySpace and started a conversation. Paris leveraged MySpace better than most, with well over 12 million plays (streams) of the four songs posted from her album. Burger King has encouraged viewers to produce and submit their own ads. With its sizeable audience, MySpace can't be ignored. But an even better conversation could be had by adding MySpace and YouTube-like social qualities to your company site. YouTube has shown us the potency of video. With a video uploaded to the site almost every second of each day, YouTube defines a new form of entertainment and a new form of communication.

Virtual worlds and online, multi-user games such as World of Warcraft are not to be ignored. It may at this moment be difficult to believe that three-dimensional (3D), immersive environments could become a part of mainstream marketing, but all indicators show this is happening. Second Life, which targets business and education, Doppelganger, a site that employs a music and entertainment focus targeted to teens, and Habbo Hotel, which has created a purely social environment for young adults, have all seen real traction. There is also Club Penguin and Nicktropolis for kids, among dozens of other virtual sites.

Second Life has over 5 million residents who spend more than $1.5 million dollars each day. (That's *U.S. dollars*, not Second Life's fictitious Linden dollars.) As in all virtual worlds, users create *avatars*, virtual representations of themselves, which interact with other avatars. It is a highly engaging format for interacting with, educating, or selling to people whom you might not otherwise be able to meet face-to-face. Entering a virtual world, however, isn't the same as producing content for any other marketing vehicle. The early-adopters who like to play in this environment need to be approached in a completely new way. The companies that have taken a grassroots approach to creating brand and reaching an audience inside virtual worlds have seen substantially better results.

The Coca-Cola Company has created Coke Studios, their own virtual world targeting promotions to teens. The Walt Disney Internet Group created Disney's Toontown Online, a virtual world targeting youngsters in a safe environment. Both Coke and Disney are leveraging virtual worlds to extend their brand. As marketers figure out how to create virtual versions of their brands, they can engage audiences in unique forums. Companies can also learn more about their product from these other-world interactions with users. And in many cases, businesses have begun to turn social interactions into purchases. Within Doppelganger, users can purchase music, videos, clothes, and other real-world merchandise.

World of Warcraft has over 8 million users. Multi-user, online games are platforms for socializing and communicating; they are no longer just video games. Teenagers grow up playing these games and enter the workforce with a natural affinity to learning in this environment. Best Buy's Geek Squad members (the computer services group) often teach and learn from each other while playing online games.[16] Virtual worlds may make it possible to do things we just couldn't do in the past. Custom systems help companies to train, plan, rehearse, and collaborate with thousands of geographically dispersed, concurrent users. Forterra Systems builds these type of virtual world applications for customers in defense, medical, corporate training, and entertainment industries.

Collecting and connecting information underlies Web 2.0 tools such as tagging, linking, and voting systems, and enable all kinds of applications or platforms that are made more functional by the people who use them. One example is spam protection software. These applications centralize and correlate all of the emails users identify as spam, then compare results to determine which emails really are spam. The software essentially counts each user's click on the "send to spam folder" button for each alleged spam, and those with enough "votes" get blocked for all users. So if you're just trying to get rid of your ex-boyfriend's emails, his emails won't get blocked from all other users of that spam protection system. The more people who use the system, the more accurate the results will be. Online tracking, data gathering, and analysis can now be inherent in your products and services, and not an afterthought.

There's data gathering, and then there is also information flow. What if you could gather up the expertise of your customers and they could learn from each other? What if customers wrote their own user stories and tutorials? It would save you resources, and you would gather a great deal more information. There are many Web sites based on this structure, including eHow.com, weHow.com, Trails.com, and WikiTravel.org. When all of your customers share their experiences, knowledge, and learning, as well as trials and tribulations, they help other people buy and use your product. Creating an environment where your users share their expertise increases the flow of information to everyone's benefit.

But there's more to the Live Web than its social, user-driven behavior. The Live Web will seamlessly incorporate next-generation technology, which will create a platform that holds the world's knowledge, behavior, interests, and desires, and connect just about every device in our home, office, or car. As the Live Web platform evolves we will be able to mine the wisdom embedded in the billions of interactions, clicks, tags, and purchases by hundreds of millions of people. Wow, this is marketing mecca! Next-generation technology will be hidden to users but the effects will be no less powerful.

Tools will be designed on top of new platforms from Radar Networks and MetaWeb (and likely others). These new software applications will allow us to automatically gather and organize large collections of knowledge. Natural language search engines from Powerset, Textdigger, and very possibly Google, will make search much more accurate and useful. The implications for applying consumer, community, or organizational knowledge to marketing will be huge. According to Nova Spivack, a Web 3.0 authority, "...more efficient marketplaces can be enabled by software that learns about products, services, vendors, transactions and market trends and understands how to connect them together in optimal ways."[17]

The Live Web will also be defined by our ability to move our entertainment and communications, and work seamlessly between devices. Slingbox makes it possible to view TV programming on your PC or cellphone. Apple TV brings videos, music, and other media from your PC to your TV. Eventually these types of tools will make it possible to view any content on multiple devices no matter where the content was first generated. Even better, super-fast, third-generation mobile networks and larger screens will turn mobile phones into the central user device for talk, music, search, socializing, price comparing, and, well, just about everything. Mobile phones will connect commonplace objects with the Internet. In Japan, McDonald's customers can point their mobile phone at the wrapping on their hamburger and get nutrition information. They can board the underground subway or an airplane using their cellphones instead of buying tickets.[18] Highly interactive billboards and magazine ads are starting to appear. Marketing messages need to adapt and mold with content as the content adapts and molds to the vehicle it is transported through.

Marketing 2.0 and the "Six Vs"

Marketing 2.0 is defined by the open, collaborative, social, virtual, user-generated, mobile environment of the Live Web. So much change in such a short time has left marketers scrambling to implement new programs with little understanding of the entire scope of activities and impact. As marketers work hard to catch up with all of the technology and change, it's time to recognize that we are marketing within a completely different medium and with a new set of rules. This book proposes a new model for marketing in the age of the Live Web.

It's time to euthanize the old marketing model, the "Four Ps": product, price, place, and promotion. Although a core section of many marketing texts taught to most marketing students, this Marketing 1.0 discipline for defining marketing strategy and planning is outdated. Consider the impact the Internet—and the Live Web—has had on each of the "Four Ps." You will see it is profound. It gives us reason to consider that the creation, management, marketing, and life cycle of a product has taken on new meaning. In direct opposition with the information posted on the marketing page of Wikipedia, I would argue with the page's editors that the "Four Ps" model is dead.

Although the "Four Ps" concepts are almost fifty years old (the paradigm was invented by E. Jerome McCarthy in his 1960 first edition text, *Basic Marketing*), many companies still organize via these disciplines. Different groups within a company are responsible for defining the product, pricing, distribution channel, and the outbound and brand marketing. Even if the groups communicate often, a deeply integrated solution is difficult at best. Innovation that spans across these disciplines is nearly impossible. It's also difficult to continuously refresh and advance the entire solution, or adapt to specific needs of the target audience or in the marketplace. Yet, all of this is mandatory in the ultra-competitive markets companies face.

The companies, constituents, and innovative gathering places that have been created by the Live Web force us to look at the marketing landscape differently. Customers and prospects talk to each other about you. *How can you participate in the conversation?* Price comparison sites destroy value add. *How can you be unique?* New marketing techniques appear to confuse the media, the message, and the consumer. *How can you be inventive, fresh, new and still build on your brand, not detract from it?* It is time to redefine the paradigm for marketing strategy, planning, and implementation.

We can no longer write a marketing plan at the beginning of the year and execute against it over the year. The traditional marketing plan can do no more than give us a snapshot of a point in time. It doesn't help us make the right decisions as we move forward in a complex and constantly changing marketplace. Marketing planning must be fluid, and I will elaborate on a new model for marketing planning in Chapter Nine.

The only marketing strategy that will work today is one that is designed to encourage and incorporate change as the product evolves. This book redefines the fundamental strategies that determine a product's success. With this thinking, it is possible for anyone to build and market products that thrive in today's extraordinarily competitive and complex marketplace. This marketing paradigm is based on the "Six Vs":

VENTURE
The deep integration of product, service, and channel of distribution

VALUE
Creating inherent "marketingness" through unique,
defendable, sustainable, and engaging value

VOICE
The perception created and the followers gained through
vision and story

VERIFICATION
Developing credibility through proof, truth, and
transparency

VICINITY
Harnessing the communities and myriad voices
of the Live Web

VEHICLE
Incorporating Marketing 2.0 strategies to attract and
delight customers

Over the next six chapters, I will elaborate on each of these strategic segments. For now, it is time to shake loose old thinking and ingrained habits. It's not enough to test the online waters; it is no longer safe to take the trusted path. The traditional tried-and-true forums for getting your message out are under attack. The way marketing has been implemented for the past forty years is dead. Marketing has been reinvented. It is exciting, inventive, and challenging, and opens many new paths for creating product successes that take off like a rocket.

2 | Think Venture

HIERARCHY KILLS INNOVATION.

It's no longer good enough to innovate once and build on it. In this interactive marketplace, great companies continuously innovate across products, business processes, and services.

It may seem overwhelming at first to encourage innovation on such a broad scale. *Are there enough smart people to come up with the ideas? How can we afford to implement all of the great ideas?* In a top-down, insular organization, people fit into their roles, do their jobs, and have little time or motivation to think out-of-the-box. "Not invented here" or "we don't do it that way" is the language of choice. In an open, porous organization, ideas flow in and out, and employees are proud to build on someone else's creativity. Management can actually create an ecosystem for innovation and execution, and each day employees will feel as though they work for an exciting, hopeful, new venture.

Whether it's Webster's definition of a speculative business or Wikipedia's definition of a daring journey, the term *venture* evokes opportunity. Venture capitalists (VC) look at a business venture as a process of managing risk. They share costs, connect entrepreneurs, and drive integration and focus. These principles—share, connect, integrate—are quickly becoming the optimal philosophies for driving organizations and their marketing in the Live Web age. Today, most businesses manage their opportunities, whether a product, service, marketing program, or customer segment, as discrete activities created and coordinated by groups formed as silos inside the company. This conventional form of management serves to limit and slow the potential of a company's opportunities.

Reaching out beyond corporate walls and engaging various audiences enables a company to build and exploit their ecosystem. Often, and without recognizing its potential, companies create ecosystems made up of employees, customers, partners, affiliates, industry analysts, and shareholders. What's changed over the past few years is that these constituents demand greater involvement and interactivity. To survive and grow, companies need to build and influence their ecosystem by offering *openness*—a transparent view of the company and an ability for outsiders to integrate or participate, *sharing*—enabling others to take part in costs, revenue, or recognition, or gain free access to intellectual property, and *collaboration*—working in real-time, interactive teams with openness and sharing.

The Live Web has given rise to a change in consumer thinking, behavior, and expectations. A product can no longer be an island unto itself. Customers look beyond the conventional definition of features, functions, instruction manuals, warranty, and service. Seamless integration of product, Web, service, support, and audience participation is now a design parameter, not an afterthought. Partly created by customers, completely transparent, inherently social, and with marketability built in, tomorrow's blockbusters will bear these trademarks.

What's more, the rules around the most fundamental of strategies—pricing—have been rewritten. Today, you have to ask, *what do I offer for free, and what do I charge for?* Ryanair gives away airline seats and charges for baggage handling. WOWIO gives away book content and earns revenue from advertisements. SpiralFrog does the same with music.[1] Lunarpages, a low-cost Web hosting service, invests heavily in live service agents, then offers superior support for free, an anomaly in the domain name service and hosting business. In the pharmaceutical industry, companies have concluded that hiring and paying nurses to sit down with customers and train them for free on how to use their product increases sales.[2] If the medical product is used correctly and positive results follow, more of the product will be used.

We build and market our products in any way that will differentiate them. We create intellectual property (IP) in order to erect barriers to entry for competitors, helping us to launch markets and solid revenue streams. This has historically been the strategy for minimizing risk. Yet, we now face tremendous competition from almost every corner of the planet. Remaining insular and depending solely on our own resources will likely doom us to failure. The Live Web is an environment that truly makes the world small and enables us to work, think, and act together in real-time. We can collaborate with partners, customers, and even strangers, expanding our knowledge and understanding of the markets, products, and opportunities around us. In what defies conventional wisdom, companies are encouraged to share some of their IP! By drawing in a more deeply involved constituency, sharing non-core assets or opening up interfaces to products can actually minimize risk, where isolation and complete self-reliance can increase it.

Marketing 2.0 drives us to think about products differently—not as a packaged item someone will purchase, but as a venture with all elements, features, service, distribution, loyalty, connectedness, evolution, and community integrated. In order to make this happen, we need to think differently, and organize and manage human resources in a way that will make all of this possible. The groups formed within this venture concept are aptly named *product team ventures*. This chapter will define how the product team venture enables a more open, collaborative, and tightly integrated solution.

This type of achievement will be hard won in the typical top-down hierarchical organization. Management often organizes teams around goals and objectives, rather than allowing teams to self-organize around ideas and passion. Typically, corporate goals and objectives close minds, while spirited philosophies open them. Companies must learn to define direction through corporate philosophies which guide and feed the minds of employees. And it is all about the product, and the people tasked to bring it to fruition. VCs know this, and it is for the most part how they determine what to fund and how to fund it. Further, to keep a venture focused, VCs dole out funds when milestones are met. They force entrepreneurs to repeatedly prove they are on the right track. That doesn't mean pulling the plug on mistakes. It does mean fostering ideas and innovation along with vigilance around markets, customers, trends, and learning. It's not a bad idea.

By one measure, the simple smallness of a start-up increases its chances of success. With the risk of failure continually around the corner, entrepreneurs are driven to spend wisely, ask for help, and turn over every stone that might lead to a win. On the flip side, the highly limited number of people involved minimizes information and ideas. Start-ups are driven to reach out—and today it is easier than ever. Through the Live Web, companies can easily tap millions of minds by opening their corporate borders and letting people in. Even if you only attract two-hundred interested parties, that's a great addition to the fifty, five-hundred, or five-thousand people you currently have. *What can these outsiders do?* They can innovate, mashup your product with other products to make new products, and share their thoughts and ideas.

Open Minds and Individual Potential

Most businesses still use a top-down managed funnel to exclude most potential products or talent in order to allow a limited set of "best" products through. Seasoned executives make the decision as to what to allow into the funnel rather than the marketplace. That's because broadcasters have limited time slots, music companies have limited budgets to promote talent, and corporations have limited human and financial resources. There are funnels everywhere you look: the half-million dollar up-front fee to get your product on a grocery store chain's shelf, the ability to excite a harried editor into publishing your book, or passing muster with a producer to get a recording contract.

The Live Web has created a work-around to the funnel. Any individual or company can make their creations available directly to the broader marketplace. Consumers generate their own entertainment and upload it to MySpace or YouTube. They mashup products and post them on free software sites. Musicians can post their music on iTunes or MySpace. And, entrepreneurs can build applications specifically to run on the social networking site Facebook at no cost to them but their time. With a passion, users create buzz to prop up a product they like. That doesn't mean bad music will sell. But if your tastes run contrary to the mainstream, you could have the opportunity to get more of what you like—say, Irish folk music.

The Live Web breaks down the barriers to getting a product to market. And although the Web encourages companies to crack open external walls, it's just as important to knock down internal walls. The conventional organization with its divisional silos puts up unnecessary barriers to producing innovative, highly integrated solutions. Marketing is spread across the organization, and includes the product development team, product marketing, corporate marketing (advertising and public relations), field marketing (sales promotions), competitive research, the channel or distribution organization with its channel marketing group, customer service, and often a separate service marketing group, too.

The reason why young companies have an advantage is because one person, or a small group, is forced to do all of these things, thereby tightening the integration between each area. It is easier for employees in small companies to have the same goal, and it's clear everyone wins if the goal is met. Corporate silos tend to compete with each other in order to push their own agenda and support their own goals often to the demise of the company.

Common at large companies, if a product group develops a better version of an older product, and it has fewer moving parts and much great mean-time-between-failure (meaning it is less likely to fail), the service contract cost goes up. *What are they thinking?* Well, the service group needs to make more money so they can hire more people and ensure the group's existence. They have a model that shows how new products create a greater flurry of service activity up front, a result which decreases significantly over time. Instead of changing the model along with a new product that is designed to reduce service activity, not increase it, the service team sticks to their guns. This hurts the customer through higher prices, and quelled innovation, as Sun Microsystems and other vendors have learned.[3] A product team venture that *owns service as part of its product development, design, and marketability strategy* is going to ensure the whole solution is simple and works best for the customer.

W. L. Gore & Associates, the company that brought us GORE-TEX®, has seven-thousand employees (or "associates" as they like to call them) and has innovated thousands of technologies and products over the past fifty-two years. *How do they do it?* One of the organizational tools they have implemented is maintaining business units that are small and fluid. *Each product team is a venture with the searing focus, fun, and creativity of a start-up.* Groups are encouraged to communicate and interact. With clear overriding principles of individual potential, product integrity, and creativity, each product group is entrusted to succeed using its own ingenuity.[4] With their venture focus, Gore has succeeded in a wide range of markets, including electronics, high-performance fabrics, and medical products by leveraging their core proprietary fluoropolymer.

Large companies often allow business units to bloat to thousands of people. This is true in the computer industry although it is well understood that software development teams made up of thousands of engineers simply don't work. If the product has ballooned to 50 million lines of code, problems will be inherent. So then, *why do so many computer companies employ such large teams, dooming them to failure (or middling success)?*

A great deal of this behavior stems from individual empire-building and the desire for command and control. An executive reigning over a large organization establishes his seniority and importance, but it's never enough. Executives keep adding to their organizations. This empire-building is a cancer in most companies, destroying the functions that keep it alive. High achievers focus on promotions, higher management positions, and larger teams. The rest of the employees are pushed into corners and smothered; rarely are they asked their opinion outside the narrow scope of their position. Much of their brain power goes to waste. You have to ask yourself which is more important: *the power gained from a bigger budget, more employees, and bigger, more complex projects, or the pride gained from the extraordinary results of innovative, successful products?* Not to mention, successful products bring a company more money, raises the stock price, and ensures employees keep their jobs. Even better, employees enjoy coming to work each day because they are on the winning team.

Another symptom of conventional hierarchy is *feature creep*, where the product team adds every possible feature over time until the product becomes big, bloated, and complex. Individuals and managers are more concerned about building the most complete, best, and biggest product. They don't even consider that it might be better to break the product into pieces and give someone else part of the pie to manage.

The product team venture needs to be given the freedom to innovate in all areas of its product's incarnation, whether it is design, marketability, integrated distribution, or another area. *Innovation* is about creating new *value*, not about creating new products. Real differentiation can come from any part of the solution not just the core technology of the *product*. The same team needs to see the product through launch, customer adoption, and product evolution.

The product team venture is not a group of individuals tasked from their silo organizations to work together. Though this is commonly the preferred process today, these "add-on" members simply bring along a predefined plan for how their part works. Instead, the product team venture is made up of a person with a service background, a person with a channels background, and so on. Each individual is a full product team venture member, and their only boss is the product team venture leader, a person whom they choose. Individuals learn to lead or follow as needed, giving the product team venture a dynamic and fluid set of behaviors. Service and channel organizations are structured so that they are able to respond to the product, service, and channel innovations that are developed. Today it is the other way around. Products are designed by the rules set by a separate service or channels group.

All of this begs the question, *how would companies ensure that there are a standard set of procedures implemented, and a required level of consistency with the company culture and creed?* The Live Web, of course. To explain, there are two things companies need today: a corporate philosophy and an institutional memory. First, consistency is critical. Consistency is not the enemy of innovation. Companies need to stand for something in their customer's minds. Employing product team ventures does not mean freedom to create complete chaos. Second, no matter how great your company is, people come and go. People are promoted or change product teams, and with them goes the brilliance and learning they put into each project.

Fortunately, we have the tools today to preserve the brilliance and learning. *How?* Through wiki pages for one (www.wiki.org). Companies can create an *OurWikibase*—a database or encyclopedia of all things that define their company. If you're not familiar with wiki, take a look at Wikipedia (www.wikipedia.org), the world's most successful wiki-based site, and the most extraordinary free online encyclopedia, or any of the following wiki sites:

- WikiTravel (www.wikitravel.org)
- ShopWiki (www.shopwiki.com)
- Wikiversity (www.wikiversity.org)
- Wikibooks (www.wikibooks.org)
- Wiktionary (http://en.wiktionary.org)

- WikiSpecies (http://species.wikimedia.org)
- WikiSource (http://en.wikisource.org)
- Wikiquote (http://en.wikiquote.org)

CustomerVision, MindTouch, Wetpaint, Stikipad, and SocialText all offer business wiki solutions (either plug-and-play software or an easy-to-use online service). Once the structure for a company's wiki intranet is set up, invited employees can create, edit, or comment on postings. The real-time company information, how-to, and how-not-to site can be available to *everyone* who needs it *at any time*. Executives or team leaders simply make it a rule that employees review the site prior to starting a project and follow any guidelines. Developing a wiki page is also a great way to discuss corporate philosophy and purpose, giving employees a deeper understanding as well as a launching pad to think creatively within the structure. Corporate standards, message architecture, and communications protocols can be set as the guidelines on the *marketingwikibase*. And marketers can be free to create while following these guides. It's amazing what employees will come up with when given a purpose and free reign to innovate within it.

How can departments within the company respond to and support the product team venture? They can focus on discovering new techniques, technologies, and processes that lower costs, increase speed to market, and add qualities that delight customers. The service organization can set up a *service wikibase* (a real-time service database or encyclopedia) for all to access, maintain a lightweight corporate organization, support the product team ventures, and of course, offer the best customer interactions.

Innovative companies are creating a corporate culture that encourages thinking outside the old corporate box, as well as the competitive box and industry box. In this way, product team ventures are free to create, think for themselves, and grab what feels right for the product, service, and partnerships they are creating. For your product to succeed in today's marketing rebirth, the flexibility to work in the product team venture environment is critical.

Let the Outside In

Of late, *co-create* has taken on new meaning in marketing. Since consumers have been producing their own videos using popular brands and posting them on YouTube, Burger King, Frito-Lay, Chevy, and Converse, among other companies, have set up contests encouraging viewers to create an ad for them. Not all companies want customers to produce their ads, but it's a good fit for some, and the concept can be extended to other marketing vehicles. Collaborating with an audience who is interested enough in your brand to take their extra time to make a video, or comment or write about it, is worth looking into further.

Most companies bring their customers in, and then ask them their opinions and input. But now we can take this process a step deeper and allow customers to take part in both the development and the marketing processes either through their ideas or actions, or by adding their own value on top. Those companies whose marketing organization masters collaboration with prospects, customers, partners, and affiliates will have an advantage over those companies that stay insular.

Collaboration enhances our ability to integrate our audience into our product up front. From sharing ideas, to creating a platform for community or discussion, or an ecosystem based on open interfaces, companies can enable *prosumers*[5] (producer/consumers), *value-add partners* (people who build something on top of your product), idea generators, message creators, or message disseminators. In all of these functions, companies can share revenue, allow others to build their own revenue model, share internal information, or share visibility and recognition.

Google offers *application programming interfaces* (APIs) (interfaces to software that make it easy to add or integrate functionality) and *open-source software* (free software that can be adapted and redistributed without legal implications), so that outsiders can participate in making Google products even better. Open APIs allow people outside a company to build something that adds value to the company's product. Sometimes third-party, add-on applications are offered free and sometimes they are designed to generate revenue.

Autodesk, a company that provides design software to engineers, has over twenty-eight hundred third-party developers creating programs that use Autodesk APIs. The result is almost two-thousand software programs (already available) that significantly increase the value and functionality of Autodesk's software platform. Facebook, in an effort to become the better MySpace, opened up its social networking platform so that users could build their own applications for fun or for revenue. Users are even allowed to generate their own ad revenue. In just the first month after the platform launched, an estimated forty-thousand users downloaded the Facebook toolkit and sixteen-hundred applications were produced. Recognizing Facebook's large and growing audience, venture capitalists are funding start-ups that build their business on top of Facebook's platform. In open markets, the more people that win, the greater the benefit to the market enabler or leader.

Openness, peering, sharing, and acting globally are the four principles introduced by Don Tapscott and Anthony D. Williams in their book, *Wikinomics: How Mass Collaboration Changes Everything*. These are the actions required of companies that will thrive in the Live Web age. According to the authors, "The old, hardwired 'plan and push' mentality is rapidly giving way to a new, dynamic 'engage and cocreate' economy."

The Live Web makes it cost-effective and simple for outsiders to participate in making your products or services successful. Reaching out and making consumers part of the development process is today's cost-effective opportunity to add value to your products. Although companies must maintain internal core competencies and an edge in developing core products, embracing resources outside the company has become an important way to create new brands, or pump up old, secondary brands.

Openness, Sharing, and Collaboration

Openness, sharing, and collaboration create a broader opportunity for innovation, constant value creation, and a prosperous feedback loop. No matter how smart your team or ad agency is, great ideas come from anywhere. Immersing your company in the marketplace will unearth more ideas and opportunities—making it possible to stay ahead of the differentiation curve. More than ever, speed counts. Engaging your audiences enables fast, intelligent decisions. Transparency and openness catalyze the process. Encouraging people inside and outside the company to interact, cross boundaries, and collaborate will help you create and sell products that appeal in the age of engage.

In the beginning of the Web, it was companies that didn't get online that fell to the wayside as the technologically adept became more available, flexible, and informative. With the evolution of the Web, it is companies that choose not to adapt to the Web's live elements by building and leveraging ecosystems, opening up their interfaces and interacting, sharing, and collaborating, that will wither away. Tapscott and Williams extend this thinking, "The companies that are the most in touch tend to be the most collaborative. And the most collaborative—the companies that are the best at creating, finding, and reapplying great ideas—are those that sustain growth over the long term."

Proprietary platforms offered by walled-off, hierarchical organizations will have a tougher go. Not so much because this strategy can't win, but because market changes make it less competitive to companies that design around openness, sharing, and collaboration. The Live Web enables companies to easily reach out to customers, partners, and prospects in new ways, making it easier to add value. According to Tapscott and Williams, "Firms that have these dynamic capabilities are most likely to be entrepreneurial, with flat hierarchies, clear vision, effective incentives, and employee autonomy."

Going forward, marketers need to determine how to make their product, service, or Web site a platform for participation. You may think "participation" and "collaboration" sound like concepts designed for the computer industry. Linux, the Apache web server, and Mozilla's Firefox browser are all peer-developed, collaborative solutions. Software is easily adapted to this model. Yet, across a wide array of product types, software is fast becoming the prime customer interface. Cars (BMW), refrigerators (LG Electronics), mobile phones (Nokia, Apple), and music players (Apple) differentiate their value through their software. If you build furniture or own a retail clothing store, your software interface is your Web site, and a place where value add can be amplified, as we will see through the Volcom example in Chapter Three.

To fully engage in Marketing 2.0, companies will need to change fundamental organizational behavior. They can do this by encouraging wide-scale interactivity and collaboration outside their corporate walls. That may require changing the way they organize and compensate employees to help employees focus on company goals, not personal outcomes. Where employees once worked hard to get promoted, they are now required to focus on innovation and collaboration with others. Management needs a new skill set around true collaboration (not delegating or outsourcing), and the ability to determine what assets can be shared.

Transparency and shared information breaks down walls between employees and management. It's no longer a question of how but of when. It's becoming significantly more difficult for companies to squelch vocal or frustrated employees. Individuals can blog and socialize on a grand public scale, sharing their gripes and concerns or revealing corporate skeletons. It simply makes more sense to encourage employees to create change, and give them an environment in which to relate, communicate, and socialize as a part of everyday business. The process of becoming open and sharing (internally and externally) will break down department silos, product silos, and people silos. This will enable an organization to leverage in real-time its collective knowledge and understanding, a process that is easy as a small start-up, but much more complex as the company grows. The limited resources and fight for survival typically found in a start-up drives a team to think and work together.

It has long been pondered how to maintain the formula that made a start-up successful as the company grows. Most often, it is people who get in the way. Corporate hierarchy and departmental silos tend to instill a walled-garden set of behaviors. Breaking down walls and thinking differently provides the opportunity to build breakthrough products. Sun Microsystems, IBM, and Apple have historically shared the same proprietary, closed system strategy. Interestingly, in recent years, we've seen astoundingly different outcomes for these three companies. *How is that possible?* Often, companies create what they are organized to build, as in Sun's case. Instead they need to be open to the unconventional, and then organize around what *will be* built, as IBM and Apple have done.

In the early 1990s, Sun Microsystems, once a high-growth, workstation company had fallen on slower times. Scott McNealy, then CEO, spent his days agonizing over how to drive the momentum back into his once high-flying company. He decided to motivate employees by talking to every person in the company, and reinforcing his vision and plan. And although the following several years would see Sun transformed into a commercial systems vendor, and reap spectacular growth once again, the evolution of the Live Web and the marketplace would later deem Sun's core strategies and objectives as failures.

The problem in the early '90s was that Sun defined itself specifically as a products company. In McNealy's motivational speech to employees, he asked, "Do we provide a product, a service, or a channel?" He compared the channel concept to a grocery store, and asked "Do we carry other companies' products on our shelves?" He went on to explain that Sun's core competencies are in building products. The company doesn't outsource its core competencies, or resell other companies' products to complete any part of its core solution. Sun doesn't pay royalties to other companies to implant what is or may become core technology. McNealy firmly believed Sun would be better off building or buying a solution—there was no middle ground. But the dynamics of the marketplace eventually changed, and the "not invented here" mindset rampant at Sun would limit their ability to execute.

When it came to paying for other companies' work, McNealy likened royalties—which today might be repositioned as sharing revenue with a key contributor—to a ransom. Partners, he assessed, could easily hold your products hostage by not delivering on features that you need, by not delivering on time, or by not delivering good quality. That is one of the fundamental reasons why Sun has built its own proprietary CPUs, operating system, and software. Historically, proprietary *has* given the company's products better reliability and the ability to differentiate. In the early 1990s, it simply wasn't imaginable that a free, open systems operating system, Web server, and browser built by volunteers could offer an even more reliable, feature-rich solution.

Yet IBM, also entrenched in proprietary, insular behavior but desperate for an operating system to compete with Sun Microsystems and Microsoft, chose a different path. The company poured deep and authentic resources into developing Linux, working with and relying on unknown engineers in the open-source community. In significantly lowering the company's development costs, and gaining positive feedback from customers who wanted much lower-cost platforms, IBM made a risky bet that paid off, and proved outside contributors can add tremendous value beyond what a company can do alone.[6] (Of course, IBM could afford multiple development efforts to hedge its bets.)

Remaining insular, Sun Microsystems and Microsoft fought the Linux movement, giving it only lip service. Rather, they continued to invest in their own proprietary platforms. Having secured hundreds (and in Microsoft's case, tens of thousands) of developers who built applications on top of their operating systems, creating huge, lucrative ecosystems, changing strategy would have been painful. Yet, openness and collaboration gave IBM a deeper understanding of customers and market dynamics, and allowed the company to embrace outsider ideas and contributions. A guiding philosophy rather than a specific strategy would have helped Sun be more open to something they didn't build themselves.

The Live Web helps companies defy conventional wisdom. Apple's strategy, although built on a proprietary system, is playing out quite a bit better than Sun's. The iPod makes a good example of how open thinking about the scope of a product can make all the difference. At first glance the iPod appears to be no more than a music player, a current-day Sony Walkman. Although a tremendous innovation at the time, the Sony Walkman, by comparison, was a simple product. It transmitted radio signals so that you could listen to your favorite radio station anywhere at anytime. It also played audio cassettes which you could go to the music store and buy.

The iPod is something altogether different. The device plays your favorite songs, albeit from a hard disk versus a tape. Yet, it is Apple's tightly integrated iTunes software and iTunes Music Store that create a platform. Not your ordinary software application, iTunes is a window—a browser, actually—to the world of music, podcasts, videos, and movies. The product is the hardware, the software, *and* the channel. iTunes and the iTunes Music Store provide the grocery-store-like shelves for music companies to provide their products. But, the opportunities here can be endless. Marketability (reinvented style, downloadable music) and accessibility (great user interfaces from the software, music store, and player) are built into the solution. Consumers can buy the product and participate in its evolution (albeit to a more limited degree than they would like).

Musicians can choose not to contract with a music company, instead selling their music directly on Apple's iTunes Music Store shelf. The iPod, which plays music, podcasts, and videos whenever and wherever its users would like, at the same time makes it possible for them to get access to music, podcasts, and videos they would never had access to before. Apple rethought convention and wasn't afraid to change the rules; in the end, they changed an industry. It's hard to knock a product that has sold over 67 million units in five years, along with a music service that has had over 1.5 billion songs downloaded.

But the Apple system is closed to music from other services and applications built by customers, even though hackers have figured out how to build and load custom applications without company approval. There is a world of innovation happening with the iPod right outside Apple's front door—and as of this writing the company chooses to ignore these opportunities. These aren't underground, jury-rigged solutions. Called *hacks* because these applications are not sanctioned by the company and void the product warranty, many are sophisticated solutions, including the porting of Linux to the iPod, called Podzilla.[7] This turns an iPod into a handheld computer and enables hundreds or thousands of applications to be built on top. Today you can get everything from games, including iDoom, iGems, Invaders, and Sudoku, to wordprocessing, custom graphics, or even a system that maps out jogging routes.

Further nibbling away at Apple's closed strategy, musicians, podcasters, and budding videographers can also offer up their creations on Web sites such as PureVolume, Heavy, LiveVideo, YouTube, MySpace, and other sites that will enable them to share revenue. The iPod's current popularity doesn't lock up the market. Creative, one of the original MP3 player companies, or another competitor could offer an open development platform, a site that aggregates and enables downloads from dozens of entertainment media sites, transparency in their business operations, and revenue-sharing with customers to draw the community away from Apple. This is what the ad network Quigo Technologies, Inc. is doing in the online ad service business. While Google and Yahoo! can't help but take notice, Quigo has made inroads by being antiestablishment, offering transparency in its ad placements, and allowing advertisers to communicate directly and build relationships with premium Web sites. Something, up until now, Google and Yahoo! have refused to do.[8]

Nikoli, the Japanese company famous for Sudoku, is a prolific producer of logic games. Instead of relying on internal resources to create their games, Nikoli accesses ideas submitted by the readers of the puzzle magazines the company publishes. The ideas are refined and tested by Nikoli, then sent back to readers for more feedback. The games that catch on are taken to market worldwide.[9] Even though the interactions don't yet occur over Nikoli's Web site, this is the Marketing 2.0 approach to creating and marketing products.

Being open, participatory, and collaborative allows for a great deal more information to permeate the company's intelligence. Today we can see the Internet has eliminated any demarcation between developer and user, marketer and customer. The linear format whereby a marketer asks a customer what they want, then requests product development add the features to the product no longer works. The customer is now an integral part of defining or creating the service offered. And this drives customers to take it upon themselves to market the product to other customers.

By today's standards, a stand-alone product is incomplete no matter how great the product performs. It is in the paradigm-changing integration of channel (the grocery store shelves), marketability (wow aspects and social aspects), customer interactivity, and serviceability that makes new products stand out. Take Digg, an online service that enables anyone to dig up news and link it to the site. Registered users of the service vote on news articles, and the ranking system shows us what is most popular at any given moment. The service is unique not only because mainstream news media all cover the same topics at the same time thereby burying interesting second tier news, but because users are empowered to drive the service and talk about the news with each other. Digg leverages the fundamental "marketingness" and conversation that is the Live Web.

In addition, Digg built marketing into the service. The company has seen almost instantaneous adoption of the "Digg This" link by a vast number of blogs and Web sites. By adding the Digg link to the articles on your Web site, readers can link your article to the Digg Web site. Recognition on Digg's front page can bring thousands of new eyeballs to your site.[10] In this process of reinventing news, Digg has set the agenda and user interface for publishing, and that hasn't been lost on other companies. Yahoo! now uses a similar voting tool for its Yahoo! Suggestion Board. Voting systems democratize information, highlight what's important to others (outside your company), and compel viewers to interact.

Most people would have thought communicating the news has been done, that there's no "new" angle, but here it is. A testimony to the success of the Digg service is its quick adoption from thirteen-thousand registered users on its opening day in 2004 to five-hundred-thousand registered users, and over 17 million visitors each month less than two years later.[11] As the Internet grows, Digg follows. The more bloggers, journalists, and pundits on the Net, the more articles users will dig up. Digg takes advantage of the biggest grocery store of writers on the planet. Even better, the service is unique, fun, and user-involved. People can't help but tell their friends.

Good strategies fail because no one has a crystal ball—markets and customers change. Having your finger on the pulse of the marketplace can transform a good strategy into a continuously evolving system that enables innovative ideas and superior execution. Actively consuming real-time information and regularly interacting with the marketplace is the answer. Tracking and analyzing every click your customers and prospects make on your Web site is critical. Logging onto forums, inviting customers to participate, reading reviews and complaints, and trolling social sites are a few of the ways to immerse yourself with data points. As Louis Pasteur said, "…chance favors only the prepared mind." Uncertainty is a part of business and should be embraced. Recognizing and managing uncertainty is a better path than demanding product teams state they are sure of the path chosen—because they never really are *sure*.

Openness, sharing, and collaboration together expose one of the biggest challenges companies face, which is defining core IP in new ways. Companies should maintain a DMZ (demilitarized zone) around IP that creates unique value and open up non-core IP to partners or the community to enable additional wealth creation. Where at one time Scott McNealy believed the only part of the company that should be outsourced was the cafeteria, today executives need to be thinking like venture capitalists and actively seeking out partners for collaboration. You can change your company by creating an ecosystem, leveraging outside resources, and focusing internal resources on inventing and reinventing in the areas where you have competence.

Dynamic Teams and Leaders

Marketing is a dynamic business. Marketing professionals become accustomed to change, uncertainty, and risk. But all too often marketers are required to fill stringent roles in controlling environments that limit creative behavior and risk-taking. It has long been difficult for companies to institutionalize innovation, creativity, and out-of-the-box thinking. The interactive and user-generated Web frees us from past limitations. It is easy and inexpensive for the people in marketing (or all employees) to learn, understand, and participate in the creation of new ideas, programs, or opportunities that break down barriers. To succeed in the age of engage, where the marketplace is cluttered and consumers hold most of the power, organizational behavior requires change.

Dynamic teams are steeped in the interactive, user-created Web. These teams come together and break apart as required by the project at hand. Employees move to new subjects easily and know how to master a new role on a new team with ease. Personal empowerment is defined by the success of the team, the project, and the learning. W.L. Gore & Associates employs a great formula. Depending on the type of solution being devised, anyone can lead, and the product team chooses their leader. *What should product team ventures do—and not do—to ensure the best ideas are heard?* Democratize information, collect wisdom from large, diverse groups, and choose a leader with passion who listens. Here's an example worth noting.

For most managers, taking absolute control over the whiteboard is a mistake—unless, of course, you're Steve Jobs. In their book, *Icon: The Greatest Second Act in the History of Business,* Jeffrey S. Young and William L. Simon illuminate how picking up a marker and writing on the board while Jobs is conducting a meeting is akin to committing career suicide. Steve Jobs is one of the few executives who can drive product success through his organization, in the process allowing few dissenting opinions and little innovation outside his plan. Jobs is one of the great conceptual thinkers. He knows where he's going and doesn't need to use trial and error to get there.

Well, that may be how it appears from the outside looking in. In reality, Jobs made huge, expensive mistakes with the original Apple Macintosh, the NeXT, Inc. computer, and at Pixar. He made these mistakes because he didn't listen, and because he wasn't open to someone else's innovative ideas. And in each case, he nearly destroyed the company. (In the case of NeXT, he did destroy the company.)

Most business owners, corporate executives, and managers will find success listening to the smart people who work around them, or thousands of miles away. Good ideas can come from anyone on the product team venture, or anywhere inside or outside of the company, from competitors and other industries, and from Web sites, books, and magazines. Corporate leaders need to define a culture that encourages ideas, and that ensures contrarian thoughts are aired, heard, and discussed. And most importantly, they need to instill in employees that speed matters.

It is the ability to hear new ideas and act on them quickly that separates the winners from the laggards. It is up to each marketing person to search out fresh thought. Quickly assessing new ideas against industry trends, competitor behavior, and your own product and marketing strategy is a good process for making decisions. The desire to innovate and push boundaries will allow new ideas to bubble up. Having real-time information at your fingertips can expedite this process and make choosing the right path much easier. Creating and innovating products and marketing in this way helps you down the path of next-generation marketing. Spending months writing reports that are outdated by the time they are finished is 1990s thinking. Open-minded collaboration is easier, faster, and more cost-effective, and leads you to Marketing 2.0.

But how can we expect teams to learn, raise the bar, and succeed in a more competitive marketplace without giving them a handbook, and educating them on mistakes made in the past? We can incorporate all of that information into the daily activity of product team ventures through wikis, thereby ensuring the team's ability to move fast, knowledgeably, and creatively in the future. The wiki can become a guide, institutionalizing corporate philosophy and educating by creating a library of institutional memories (failures and successes).

By exploiting individual potential and opening minds to thinking beyond tradition or convention, ideas will abound. *How do you filter all of the ideas coming through?* One way is to ask three simple questions: *What do I think? What do I know? What can I prove?* In this way, you can determine how much risk there is with the idea as part of the evaluation. What you think is often determined by your intuition, based on all of the learning you've experienced up to that point. What you know is assured by facts and figures that back up your ideas, but facts aren't enough. You must verify through market experience, customer interactions, and alternative ideas.

Look at the highly productive venture between PepsiCo and Starbucks which offers ready-to-drink coffee products. The successful collaboration opened up an entirely new channel for Starbucks—the grocery store shelf, and a new market for Pepsi—coffee drinks. Each company brings its area of specialty to the joint venture which has become the leading provider of bottled coffee drinks. In fact, Pepsi has deployed a quick-learning process that has enabled the company to move swiftly into *non-carbonated* drinks, while Coke with their long-drawn-out analyses hasn't been able to execute.[12] Pepsi is now the leading provider of bottled water (Aquafina), sports drinks (Gatorade), enhanced water (Propel), chilled juice (Tropicana), and bottled tea (Lipton, through a joint venture). Pepsi management deploys decisive action, leveraging its own or outside strengths. Today, companies whether large or small require small teams that can create, evaluate, and move fast. As Jason Jennings and Laurence Haughton so aptly named their book, *It's not the BIG that eat the SMALL, it's the FAST that eat the SLOW.* The authors, in considering both good decisions and bad decisions, determine it is better to make a bad decision that you learn from than take too long to make a good decision. According to Jennings and Haughton, "The fast thinker has a good memory, learns from previous experiences and always learns from failure including the unexpected failures that occasionally take place."

Marketers now build webs of value creation through ecosystems that consist of prospects, customers, prosumers, affiliates, or a mix of these groups. Broadening the definition of value helps businesses take charge of the dynamic changes across marketing. No longer can marketers rely on a single unique value to differentiate their product. Rapid re-innovation and creative thinking as well as a good understanding of market changes are required. Companies need to determine if a product is to be reinvented or killed, and eliminate the cash cow strategy. *Cash cows*, the marketing term referring to an older product whose growth has slowed but whose higher margins enable extra cash to be invested in new products, have a bigger purpose now. They can be used to learn more about customer behavior, and opened up to customer creativity and interaction. If we think about our cash cows in innovative ways, they can become new again. Otherwise, they are sapping resources that would be put to better use on a growth opportunity.

Data and Decision Making

Risk is inherent in marketing. There are simply too many choices, and no definitive mathematical model will help you choose the right course. However, continuously accessing real-time data and social interactions common on the Live Web have changed the process for intelligence-gathering. Turning data into useful information in which to base decisions has become easier through open dialog, and through *decision markets*—communities created for people to wager on the likelihood of a future event or the value of an idea, product, or feature for the purpose of making predictions. Decision markets can help you get at the right answers faster. There is untapped wisdom in every organization, and certainly outside of it for you to exploit.

Real-time market intelligence is one of the defining attributes of Marketing 2.0. At no point in our history could we know as much about our customers, prospects, competitors, market trends, and other global or economic factors instantaneously. Mining the data is fairly easy using RSS, Ajax, or other technologies. Exposing entire organizations to this wide-scale information, and developing a platform for conversation and learning has never been easier than now, with the advent of wikis. Marketing organizations must be on a constant drive to learn, test their assumptions, adjust, and move forward. Leonard Fuld discusses how to excavate and pinpoint useful market and competitive data in his book, *The Secret Language of Competitive Intelligence*. In determining how to quantify the unquantifiable, Fuld says, "Intelligence is about making critical decisions while balancing imperfect, but reasonable, knowledge with a degree of risk." He goes on to explain how crucial it is to see your competitors and the marketplace realistically, and to act on that knowledge whether or not the picture is perfectly clear.

The fact that we can quickly access so much more data shouldn't weigh decision-making down. Waiting for the perfect picture means a slow, agonizing death. Gathering the right information, and demanding of your organization to see it realistically and not through a narrowed lens, is critical. Hewlett-Packard (HP) did just that when the company refocused its printer division on the emerging digital imaging market. When the company started heavily marketing their new focus, the home digital image printing market was all but nascent. This was an unlikely choice for a Fortune 500 company and a risky bet. Yet, the company saw what could be a billion-dollar-plus market opportunity and jumped on it before any of their competitors (who all had the same information) even noticed.[13] Being first is good.

The job of each marketer is to access and evaluate every possible bit of market data in real-time to make fast, intuitive decisions. Almost anything can be found on the Internet today. If you search and can't find it yourself, there is likely a Web-based company that has aggregated the information for you. And even better, with RSS you can have all of that information sent to your desktop in real-time. RSS is the quintessential tool marketers should now depend upon. Choose an RSS reader (Newsgator, Pluck, Google Reader, Feedlounge, Bloglines, Netvibes, My AOL). These hosted applications make it quick and easy to add live feeds from bloggers, online magazines, online newspapers, social sites, competitor's sites, analysts, and pundits. It is so important to glean at least a little information each day that scanning industry and competitive news should become a part of everyone's morning ritual.

Do you know every blogger that comments on your industry? To track trends or weigh the positions bloggers are taking on any subject, you can check out Technorati, Blogpulse, Alexa, or IceRocket. You can learn a great deal about your competitors' Web-site marketing, and behavior of customers on their Web sites, by looking them up in Hitwise or ComScore (for a fee), Alexa's traffic tool or even through Jim Boykin's SEO (search engine optimization) tools (http://www.webuild-pages.com/seo-tools/). Boykin's Top Competitor or Strongest Subpages tools will tell you who ranks highest for a particular keyword or which of your competitor's site pages is the most popular or the most linked to. You can search Amazon, Shopper.com, BazaarVoice, Yelp, or Trust-edOpinon to see what customers are saying about your competitors' products or service. Or for that matter, determine how much they are being talked about (if at all).

Sometimes, though, that isn't going to be enough. You may be at a crossroads, or learned that a competitor is doing something that will impact your product. The best method to quickly think through complex or confusing issues is to encourage open debate within your organization or even set up a formal debate on a directed topic. Get at the core information. *What are the competitors doing? What might they do? Will the economy have an impact? What hasn't been tried in this market or product space? What is the most common customer problem and how could we solve it in a completely new way? What is the one value-add that would separate our product from the pack?* Organize a brainstorming session where everyone invited brings new information to the table, and all ideas are openly discussed. Fuld teaches his clients to implement a formally organized war game. This more structured process can open your eyes to events you may not have considered before.

Decision markets are an option, too. Introducing decision markets in his book *The Wisdom of Crowds*, James Surowiecki defines how crowds can be tapped for their collective knowledge, giving us an accurate picture or at least a better answer than we could likely find on our own, no matter how many experts we hire. In order for decision markets to work, Surowiecki states that there are three conditions that must be met: diversity, independence, and decentralization. He also clearly articulates under what circumstances crowds do not offer an accurate picture. Small companies or groups who have been together for a while won't offer enough diversity. When people follow the crowd (i.e., the behavior that led to the tech bubble burst in the stock market), the requirement for independence (independent thinking) is missing.

But in groups that meet the required elements, Surowiecki shows how useful a decision market can be. Several real-world businesses have been built on this concept including Marketocracy, a Web-based investment firm, A Swarm of Angels, a cult film project, and Crowd-spirit, an inexpensive electronic device company. Hewlett-Packard set up a decision market employing just fifteen employees from finance to help better forecast the company's services business in the first month of the quarter. The finance people bought and sold virtual stock that represented various forecasts. The result was a fifty-percent improvement in operating-profit predictability over the forecasts completed by individual managers.[14] IBM, although not employing a decision market, has built a system to mine over six billion documents on the Web in order to answer market research or corporate branding questions.[15] They have also used their system to determine the popularity of TV shows or music. By analyzing behavior on college music Web sites, IBM has been able to predict songs that would hit the top of the pop charts—better than the industry market research firms.

The point is that decision markets are another quick and useful technique to get good data points. In this way you can make decisions more quickly. Since marketers face a number of complex decisions with regard to unique value, market segments, customer behavior, marketing messages, brand, and trends, tapping every known facility to make better decisions makes sense. What you don't want to do is set up a competitive intelligence team separate from your key marketers. The best asset a marketer has is his *intuition*. Great intuitive thinkers develop what appears to be a natural skill through a wide variety of experience and continued learning. Marketers need to continually build up their instincts.

Instead of the traditional process of marketers writing a specification and handing it over to product development to respond, they can run a debate or war game to get all the data out on the table, and encourage opposing opinions. Organizations need to learn to let go of sacred cows and listen, and embrace outsider input. Next, they can assess the risks by being honest about what they don't know. With this new process, companies can move quickly, and more easily adjust as the landscape changes.

What do you do if your organization doesn't have enough diversity, breadth, or depth to create a provocative debate? You can go outside the company and ask for help; target the people who are already talking about your company. Additional options include enlisting a university or graduate school class, or posting a contest on your Web site. Do what it takes to get fresh, provocative ideas into your marketing and product planning. This will help you innovate, create, and differentiate, enabling your company to stand out from the pack.

3 | Value Reborn

IF YOU HAVE NOTHING UNIQUE, YOU HAVE NOTHING AT ALL.

Although there are several attributes to a successful value proposition, nothing is as important as the *core uniqueness*, or what it is that makes your product or service stand out in the marketplace. "Me too" products have nothing to say for themselves, or their companies. You can make money riding on another company's coattails (and innovations), but you can't become great.

It can be hard work finding the core of what makes your product unique. And sometimes you don't even know it's there until outsiders point it out to you. This chapter will take you through the process of unearthing your product's core, unique value, but first, let's take a look at all four attributes that make up a persuasive customer value proposition. The persuasive value must be *unique, defendable, sustainable,* and *engaging.* There's a fifth attribute pertaining mostly to business-to-business products, and that is *measurability*, a concept covered in Chapter Five. The end-goal is to define, support, and differentiate value in such a way that customers will pay *more* for your product or substantially more customers will *desire* your product over that of the competition.

There are many choices for how you can create value either through technology, services, online community, open interfaces, meeting a specific need, employing a new business method, reducing costs (and price), or following a strong belief system. Your differentiated value can lock customers in, invite them to participate, and create unparalleled loyalty. Whether unique value is intrinsic to the product design, services added on, or customization for a specific market segment, you will know it connects when it surprises and delights customers or fills a clear need. Let's take a closer look at examples for the four attributes of a persuasive customer value proposition.

Unique

A value that is unique clearly differentiates a product from the competition. Lunarpages's exceptional customer service in the hosting business, HBO's out-of-the-box, ultra-creative programming, Costco's return policy, and Ryanair's free or unbelievably cheap airline seats are all examples of unique, differentiated value.

Defendable

Unique value is defendable when competitors cannot easily duplicate it. To ensure unique value remains defendable, companies need to build and continuously invest in competencies that grow and extend the differentiating value, so that competitors cannot catch up. Smart companies rethink, question, and reinvest in an established value in order to stave off competition and upstarts. Technological barriers such as Google's PageRank algorithm and Palm Pilot's Graffiti software are difficult to recreate. Costco can absorb product returns up to a year after purchase because of the company's business practices with its vendors, cost controls, and a loyal customer base. Few companies even try to match their policy.

Sustainable

For a value to be sustained, companies will need to continually expand on their differentiating factors by enhancing them, adding to them, opening them up to outside innovation, and driving the value into every part of the organization. If the entire company creates business processes around the differentiating value including accounting practices and vendor interactions, then all facets of the business add to the unique value and help sustain it. This is what Patagonia does with its differentiating value for offering high quality, multi-use, environmentally-conscious, sporting apparel. They demand these features are an intrinsic part of their fabrics, vendor relationships, finished products, and marketing.

Engaging

There has long been car fanatics, music enthusiasts, and hobbyists of every sort. Products that engage and customers who get involved isn't a new phenomenon. The movement, however, has grown from the excited few to the masses. Products that engage are interactive, delightful, and "sticky." They keep customers coming back for more. And often, they offer interesting options for people to get involved. The iPod is a product and a service that keeps us interacting with Apple and talking to our friends. We want to build on it, customize it, and even create personal content to play on it. It is made to engage.

You don't have to look far to see many companies that go to market without first defining a unique value for their product or service. Products are often launched with hopes that customers will figure out why they want to buy it. This happens often in hot markets, where one company is winning big and dozens of other companies jump in, hoping to cash in on the popularity of the product category.

With Apple's introduction of the iPod and the ensuing growth of the digital player market, several companies entered the market or seriously upgraded their previous offerings.[1] *What makes Microsoft's Zune interesting to anyone? What about Creative Zen Vision or Samsung YEPP? Who are they targeting? What unique value offers strong enough appeal to pull buyers away from Apple, the clear leader, and buy*

*something else? Could it be price, a better screen, longer battery life, or
the ability to download content from multiple Web sites?* None of these
attributes have legs (they can't be sustained), nor do they create a broad
enough community around the product to impact the iPod audience.

Entering an established market requires rethinking what the leader
is doing and not doing. In fact, when analyzing competitors, it is critical to think about what they are *not* doing—at all or well enough—instead of what they are doing. This will help your product connect with
a group of dissatisfied or not yet engaged customers. Microsoft chose
to get a copycat music player to market quickly rather than create a
product that would attack the iPod's weakness, namely it's proprietary,
closed nature. The goal is to create your own space, attract your own
audience, and develop a deep and long-lasting relationship with customers. When you do this, your product will rise above the din of marketing messages.

Five Things You Must Know About Value

Developing a unique and persuasive value proposition is one of the
most difficult of all marketing activities. That may be why so many
companies go to market without one. Before we start down the path of
developing a unique value proposition, there are five things you need
to know about value.

1. If your product has no unique value, you will be
    selling on price alone
2. If you create real or perceived value, you can ask a higher
    price and get it
3. Free can be a great value
4. You cannot lie about value
5. A value proposition is not a list of benefits

Although most of us know these to be true, it is worth a moment to
remind us of the fundamentals, and so we explore each in detail.

If Your Product Has No Unique Value, You Will Be Selling on Price Alone

There are two meanings of the term value. First, there is intrinsic value—what we like about a product. Second, there is the value we place on a product, or in other words, its price. Price and intrinsic value are uniquely tied. If you can define the value of your product, and it differentiates your product from your competitors as well as meets a perceived or real customer need or desire, you can set a higher price. Price in many cases is defined less by demand and more by a defensible value position. Customers are happy to pay more for iPods, groceries from Whole Foods Market, Waterford crystal, and private school.

It is virtually impossible to combine unique value with lowest price, because each of these approaches requires a complete business model to back it up. There is an old adage in marketing, "Don't walk down the middle of the road or you will get run over." Companies must explicitly choose a side to walk on. In other words, your product sells on value or it sells on price. You can't do both.

If you sell on price, your margins can be razor-thin, providing you with less funds to invest in future products or differentiating value. More importantly, your product is likely to be viewed as a commodity by your customers—they bought the *cheap* digital player, mobile phone, or PC. The price matters not the brand. You can see this problem playing out in the commodity Web-site hosting business. The companies offering the most storage space, domains, and subdomains, and the highest transfer speeds with the lowest price provide the worst service. In fact, several of the most expensive vendors still provide the worst customer support. Yet, Lunarpages has found a way to offer a good set of features—not the biggest or best—with a good price (about middle of the pack) and differentiate themselves through spectacular customer care, something a large segment of customers value. The more customers their great service and support attracts, the more funds they have to invest in this differentiating feature.

Motorola tried to combine low price and high value with the RAZR mobile phone. The phone was introduced at a price of $499, but over time it was reduced to just $49 likely as part of an effort to grab market share.[2] The company had funded a high value, branding campaign that focused on the original name and unique, thin style of the phone. The low price combined with high-value, high-cost marketing sent Motorola walking squarely down the middle of the road. And it wasn't long before they were slammed with a billion-dollar revenue shortfall, and phone margins that had dropped by more than fifty percent. To recover, Motorola has reinvented its strategy to focus on high value (feature-rich), high margin (high priced) mobile phones, as well as spend its marketing dollars wisely by establishing one or two brands instead of spreading dollars across several brands and marketing activities.[3]

You can create a business model around a product or service that is focused on offering the lowest price as the differentiating value just as Southwest and Ryanair have done in airline travel, and as USA Today has done in news. These companies market the persuasive value proposition of a high-value product or service without the bells and whistles at the "lowest price" or "free," and customers eat it up. Even though they are in a high-value business, their low-cost business models make the low prices viable. And their lowest-price strategy segments the market, attracting those customers that are happy to receive less service or fewer features for a much lower price. Squeezing margin on a high-cost product is inauthentic, as Motorola learned, and won't have the same effect. The high-value product will engender a *commodity* or *cheap* image, and the high cost to build and maintain added value and substantial marketing can't be sustained.

Pencils, wheat, and the wood used to build your home are commodities. When it comes to commodity products, every competitor or alternative can easily replace what you sell. Competitive price wars are likely. And worse, your customers will constantly beat you down on price. This is a tough way to make a living. And as we've seen in the PC business, often you can't. If you sell on price alone you probably want to figure out a way to change your product.

Ink is a commodity—or so you would think. Printer companies figured out how to change the rules for this commodity by packaging it in a proprietary plastic container. They focus their value sell on a highly featured printer/scanner/fax machine (although most are not well differentiated). Interestingly, the high-value printer is sold fairly cheaply in order to lock the customer into continuously purchasing their proprietary commodity ink at a premium price—the only ink package that fits into the printer purchased. The customer buys a printer and pays a high royalty on it every time they need ink. If all printers were forced to use a standard plastic package to hold the ink, the price of ink for your printer would go down dramatically. (That isn't likely to happen.) Recently, Kodak entered the market with a new printer, and *what do you think is their differentiating value?* Cheap ink.[4]

At Universal Forest Products, the company buys raw lumber and resells it to businesses that build residential or commercial buildings, or companies such as Home Depot or Lowe's that then resell to consumers. Although there are many types of wood products, most lumber companies can get access to almost all of them and provide them at the same or lower price. Lumber is a commodity. So, the business becomes largely about streamlining process and reducing cost in order to offer the lowest cost to customers. In order to move up the value ladder, Universal Forest Products now pre-fabricates sections of the home, making it quicker and easier for construction companies to build a home. Much of the pre-fabrication is custom, so Universal Forest Products can charge more for the finished product than the cost of the parts used. Construction companies will pay the price because time to market in completing a home is highly valued. An added benefit is that construction labor costs are reduced.

IBM has faced margin pressure in their services business, which accounts for over fifty-percent of the company's revenue, from India-based outsourcing companies Infosys, Wipro, and Tata Consulting Services. The low-cost competitors enjoy a much lower cost business model, and the pricing-pressure has driven IBM upstream. The company's response has been to offer higher value, more expensive research, software, and services that require specialized skills, and to better use skills across the company no matter where they are located. The changes have given IBM's profits a boost.[5] Adding value to your product or service can get your company out of the price-war arena.

If You Create Real or Perceived Value, You Can Ask a Higher Price and Get It

Creating a unique, highly differentiated product makes it possible to increase the price. A product with unique, defensible value can ask a higher price because there is no alternative (or no perceived alternative). Even in a market where alternatives to your product exist, you want to define a value in such a way that your competitors don't appear to have it. You want to focus your product development team's energy on increasing the capabilities of that value, making it more difficult for others to compete on that value. In other words, you want to stay ahead of the curve.

Toyota introduced the low-cost hybrid automobile with the Prius. The car reaped the benefit of U.S. government-sponsored consumer incentives, such as tax credits and allowance to drive in the carpool lane without requiring a passenger. Getting to market first and continually refining their technology has established Toyota as the clear leader in this segment of the market (which charges several thousand dollars more for the hybrid model than the standard model).[6] In fact, other car companies have chosen to license the technology from Toyota rather than try to catch up ensuring Toyota's continued leadership.

A proprietary technology or proprietary business model such as Apple's iTunes Music Store which only works with the iPod player enables the company to defend its unique value, maintain a high price, and lock-in customers. The proprietary ink cartridge produced by HP which only works in HP printers maintains the high price of ink. Image alone can enable a company to demand a higher price than the competition. *Branding*, or substantiating a specific perception of a product, is critical to defining a market space and separating from the pack—just look at Waterford crystal, Smith & Hawken outdoor furniture, or Hermes Birken bag (purse). The image developed by these products is sustained beyond the advertising and branding the companies do. We also see this effect in the long-ingrained, high-quality image of German-built automobiles which has kept prices high year after year for BMW and Mercedes.

Creating and communicating differentiated value enables the customer to justify spending more. If you can prove to your customers that they will save money, save time, be more competitive, or fix an issue they face daily, or you can define a class of service or quality of life associated with owning your product, you will be able to charge more than your competitors. If your competitors cannot provide the same value, you can hold your prices high for a longer period.

Price, however, is impacted by company behavior and activities in the marketplace. Although demand may continue to increase for your product, the price may have to go down due to competition or the threat of competition. The price may decrease because you haven't defended your value position by continually adding features, partnerships, or whatever it takes to increase or recreate your product's unique value.

Free Can be a Great Value

Music videos used to be free. They were given to MTV to promote artists. Today music companies want compensation if music videos are uploaded to social sites including YouTube or MySpace.[7] The music elite have missed the boat. Google provides free use of its Gmail email program, word processor, and spreadsheet software. MySpace, You-

Tube, and Digg are free to use. *USA Today* provides its online news for free. *Why?* So they can attract masses of customers who will purchase something else (just as music videos were designed to entice consumers to buy the musician's CD). Although the online advertising model can only support so many businesses, there are alternative means to creating revenue streams. In the age of the Live Web, free is effective.

It may be the core product you should give away free in order to attract the largest possible audience, or it could make more sense to give the extras away for free. One of the most frequently used words for online search, *free*, is viral. Clearly, if you build tractors you're not likely to be giving them away for free. Yet, you can create community and attract prospects by giving away services, information, or after-market products.

It's not that you should be giving up revenue, but looking at alternative revenue streams. You have to ask, *what would delight my customers if I gave it to them free, and what wouldn't they mind being charged for?* You may consider creating new or add-on products that add value (either to give away free or charge for). *Is support value-add?* No. If a customer buys your product and can't use it without calling you, then you owe it to them to help, no matter how many times they have to call to get it right. That doesn't mean you get to provide terrible support— long call wait times, even longer email responses, or poorly trained support people. Go ahead and charge for any extra, higher value service you can think of such as professional services, but support your customers well and for free.

That is, unless you choose to give the product away for free and charge for support and other services. Ryanair, which you will read about in detail in Chapter Seven, charges for baggage handling, and offers insurance and other products on their Web site to provide additional revenue streams and offset the cost of a free or very cheap seat. This kind of out-of-the-box thinking has built their business beyond all imagination. SpikeSource, a technology services company, doesn't charge for their product only for their services. They have built a sophisticated testing and configuration management platform for open-source software. Their high-value platform is free and the open-source software is free, and they charge corporate customers for management and support services.

Many Live Web companies offer their product or service for free and build their revenue stream through online advertising. The online advertising revenue model is all about the largest possible audience who visits long and often. Not every product or service is going to attract millions of customers or prospects, or be able to sustain a business through ad revenue.

If your Web site is the key software interface you offer to your customers, create an environment where they have reason to visit daily by offering free information, reports, tools, communications, and community. Engage them. This will attract prospects to your space and give customers a reason to come back often. You should ask users what they're looking for that they didn't find, and ask them if they want to pay for it. You may be surprised by the ideas and revenue streams that could materialize. Craigslist uses this model. The classified ads Web site, which is free to users, asks its users what they would like to see added to the service. They ask users if they would like link ads, or if the company should do more outbound marketing and sales. Users drive the content on the site and they help police the site.[8] What a great way to attract and keep customers.

You Cannot Lie about Value

What is real? The product perception or image that offers something that I (the consumer) desire is real to me, as long as the product itself lives up to its image. A BMW is sexy; a Volvo is not. If you tell me you make my home secure with your product, then you must execute on that value. LukWerks digital surveillance cameras promise to secure customers' homes. So the system needs to continuously work. In this case, the keys to success are quality control and service. If the power supply to the camera dies, service needs to ship a working power supply to the customer, no questions asked. Having to call the company twice, fill out forms, and plead with service to send the new power supply prior to the company's receiving the broken one back, breaks the model. While the camera is down, the customer's security is down. If customers don't feel safe with a security product, the value is lost.

If you have built a company reputation on performance and reliability, and you drive that value and its story across your company and out to your audience, you are building a trust with your audience. Intel did this with their "Intel Inside" campaign. Breaking that trust destroys credibility. Intel found this out in 1994, when they tried to hide a flaw in the Pentium processor that caused a mathematical error in a narrow set of circumstances. They chose not to tell the public—but the Internet speeds information flow, and bad news travels fast. A single person discovered the chip's flaw and emailed a few people, who ran their own analyses, and in just twenty-four days the substantiated information passed from online newsgroups and emails to the mainstream press. Today, with blogs and social sites, this public outing of a company's mistakes, and further pick up from mainstream press happens within a day or two, sometimes in just a few hours. Still, Intel chose initially not to recall the chip. The backlash was scorching. Intel was knocked off its pedestal, and the company has never regained its position. The Live Web implores you not to lie, or else.

Whatever you do, build a marketing foundation based on real competencies, an intelligent strategy, and a believable view of the future. Then support your claims through consistent behavior across the corporation.

A Value Proposition is Not a List of Benefits

If you go to a tradeshow and pick up a dozen brochures or data sheets, *what do you see? Are the companies offering clear, unique value, or a list of benefits?* Amazingly, nine times out of ten, it's a list of benefits. If you are stating the same value as your competitors, *how do customers know who to call?* Too often the marketing team determines what customers want to buy, then restates the list of needs as benefits of the product. It's simply the easiest thing to do. The problem is that the benefits list will likely be the same as your competitors' lists. Customers then will have no specific reason to choose (or even remember) your product.

If you talk to your customers to determine what benefits are important, you can fall into a hole that limits your vision. Customers define to a limited extent what it is they want, because they aren't focused on dreaming up what is possible. *They* are trying to solve a current problem. *You* are trying to change a marketplace. As in Henry Ford's oft-quoted comment, had he asked his customers what they wanted, they would have told him, "a faster horse." It is critical to push your thinking *beyond* benefits. You must determine what is of value to your customers that is based on your company's core competencies. You then focus your energy and determination on making that core value the heart of everything that you do, from partnerships to service and support.

As if creating unique value isn't already difficult enough, it is becoming much harder. It is no longer enough to create value once, then grow and extend the product until its cash-cow days. The Internet lowers the cost of entry so dramatically that competitors can come from just about anywhere. Companies can also market products with similar messaging even though the products aren't direct competition, thus cluttering up the air space.

Sometimes a product or service meets a need so well that people are drawn to it, as was the case with Google Search, Digg, and Starbucks. Word of mouth and repeat business were enough to launch these ideas. Momentum often keeps a product or service popular unless the company loses focus or the market changes. Consumer values change over time, and competitors come out of nowhere with a new model for doing business. Unique value must be reborn on a regular basis. Tracking the changing nature of consumer behavior and the entry of competitors or alternatives is now more feasible for even the smallest company using Web 2.0 technology and is required for survival. Real-time information analysis is a make-it or break-it function of all marketing organizations, enabling them to continually rethink and re-create value.

If you can prove out the value of your product and separate your product from the competition, then your customer will *want* to pay more. Proof can be in the customer experience with your product, in an analysis tool that incorporates the customer's business complexity and illustrates what your product can do, or it can be in a competitive comparison or even a third-party attribution if the customer holds the third party in high esteem. Of course, product momentum in the marketplace is the best proof. With aggressive competition, it isn't enough to put a great product on the market and list its benefits. You must be able to articulate unique value and back it up with *proof*.

There are several paths you can take to create or uncover unique value. Most companies should start by evaluating internal core competencies that can be leveraged as unique value and more importantly, create barriers to entry for competitors. Another option is defining and redefining unique value based on market trends, and competitor and customer analysis. The third option is to engage partners, customers, and interested parties to participate in creating and re-creating value.

Unique Value and Barriers to Entry

Apple has a core competency in innovative product design and tackling innovation challenges. Dell has a core competency in built-to-order, just-in-time business processes. Sun Microsystems has a core competency in system networking and throughput. Google has a competency in scaling software and storage systems (that's how they manage the explosive growth of data and media on the Internet without glitches and downtime), as well as search algorithms. For many years, these companies have transformed these core competencies into values, and defended and sustained them. And for a period of time, each of these companies has delighted their customers. However, once a company allows their competitors to encroach upon the competency or the unique value they provide, or the company no longer re-creates value, they lose their leadership position.

Core Competency	Value Proposition	Messaging

What exactly does core competency mean? It is an established, deep, and complete capability in one or more specific disciplines. A *core* competency is embedded deep within your employees or processes. It is the starting place for building unique value and staking a unique place in the minds of your audience through your communications. It's a simple concept that takes a great deal of work to execute.

Core competencies are the building blocks over which unique value is created. A deeply-developed competency inside your company can create a significant barrier to entry for your competitors. In other words, it can stop competitors from catching up with you. The quicker you extend and expand upon your competency, the harder your competitors will have to work. And your customers will believe you have unique value no one else can offer. Competencies range from technical acumen, quality, and service to advanced business processes. The goal is for your company to be so good at some element of the product, service, or business that no one compares. For well over a decade this stood true for IBM in professional services and Dell in direct sale, built-to-order, low-cost business processes.

But, it's not enough to develop and exploit a core competency. That competency must be defended and sustained over time, and that takes investment, innovation, and focus. In the ideal world, your core competencies transform into a clear, unique value proposition of which you then communicate to the world. Google's value proposition is also the company's goal. Making the world's information available and accessible sounds simple but requires a slew of competencies and continuous growth and development.

So far, Google is the best search company to execute against the value as stated, but they are far from actually meeting it. Offering this value would be unique since a great deal of information isn't on the Web yet (and someone needs to get it there). And because search algorithms aren't yet good enough (as of this writing) to understand the semantics we use when we search—often we don't get the exact results we're looking for. Moreover, as various handheld devices and a new category of products (TVs, refrigerators, cars, etc.) connect to the Net, information will need to transform before it arrives. Most Web sites are still useless if read from a mobile-phone display. Making the world's information accessible is Google's mantra, but they must continue to innovate against this unique value, or they have left the door open for another company to leapfrog their efforts.

As companies grow, it is easy to lose focus on the competency that created their initial success. Competencies are a sensitive feature of any organization. You can grow, expand, and innovate on a competency you've mastered, but if you push too far outside your competency boundaries the results can be disastrous. The business press report all too often on companies that reach beyond their core competencies by buying a business they know nothing about, or entering a market where they don't have enough knowledge or experience. With acquisitions, one of the key problems is the difficulty in fully integrating or aligning another company and its products so that the merged companies have the same (albeit bigger and better) DNA—the genetic building blocks of the company. Without that, the products from the acquisition tend to flail, not getting the creative energy or focus needed to compete in the marketplace.

Companies often naively enter markets where they have no background, strengths, depth, or advantage. Microsoft did this when they entered the music-player market with Zune, and Sun Microsystems did it when they entered the desktop business software market with StarOffice. Sun's goal was to create a business software service hosted on backend servers and accessed over the Internet by desktop users for free, a good strategy that was the antithesis of Microsoft's desktop applications. However, to win with this strategy Sun had to build several competencies at one time, including collaboration with the open-source community, office software, desktop applications, service over the Internet, and support services. Even a large company will struggle while trying to tackle all of these together.

First, Sun purchased a software company and their software didn't already offer the key function—service over the Internet. Then management demanded all employees start using StarOffice, a suite of tools not ready for primetime. Employees balked, setting a negative tone around the application. In order to get outside help to rescue the project, Sun renamed the software OpenOffice, and offered it to the open-source community by creating OpenOffice.org. Yet, instead of developing a competency in collaboration and learning the ways of the peer-community, Sun projected its leadership over the group and positioned the company as the major contributor (which continues today).

The weak response from the OpenOffice community (compared to Firefox, Linux, and others), as well as Sun's lack of competency in desktop software, has limited the impact of StarOffice on the marketplace. While IBM chose to change their traditional, insular behavior and invest correctly in building a new competency in collaboration and open source, Sun has not been able to control their NIH (not-invented-here) mindset. In seven years, OpenOffice has had little material impact on Microsoft, and today a new set of players—Google, ThinkFree, Soho, and Transmedia—have developed software-as-a-service over the Internet, and will try to unseat Microsoft's desktop software stronghold with a grassroots process.

As you might expect, the bigger the company, the greater number of competencies they will develop. Small companies must have at least one competency in order to succeed. Most often the issue isn't figuring out what one competency a company has, it's determining among all the great things a company is doing, which is actually a competency that matters. Lunarpages has built a competency in service geared to the single-person company with little resources, time, or technical knowledge. Without evaluating core competencies, companies often market value they cannot differentiate from the competition.

To uncover your core competencies, you will need to go through a thorough examination of the people, products, technologies, business processes, and any other ingredients your business employs. You may find your core competencies are not unique to your market. So the question becomes, *how can you apply your competency in unique ways to create unique value or go after unique opportunities?* Dell's business processes allow customers to configure PCs on the fly, evaluate or compare prices, and purchase on the spot with delivery in just days. It took over ten years for competitors to come close to their proficiency with these processes. *Could it be a process you've developed that makes your product or service different or special?*

When identifying core competencies, leave no stone unturned. You are not just developing a laundry list. You are going to determine what will drive and sustain your competitiveness. As you look at core competencies and determine which ones rise to the top of the list, you need to then determine how to establish that competency across the company and how you will continually reinvent and strengthen the value. *Is it possible your company doesn't have any core competencies?* Not likely. It is possible, however, that your products look just like your competitions'. If your company's core competencies aren't unique in your industry or aren't strong enough to build unique value, then you have a few choices:

1. Invest in developing a core competency that will differentiate your company.
2. Focus on a niche segment of the market where you can stand out from the more general features and knowledge of the competition.
3. Reinvent your products.

Investing in a core competency can be as simple as providing training for some of your key employees. It can be in hiring the best and brightest in the value expertise you are building, and it can be in determining how to extend your core competency into new areas as W.L. Gore & Associates does so well. As mentioned earlier, the company's competency in fluoropolymers has enabled Gore to create exceptional brands, including GORE-TEX and Glide dental floss, as well as enter a variety of markets from electronic components to medical devices. Gore has figured out how to sustain their value by continuing to reinvest in their core competency. In addition, a core competency can be extended into new markets as Amazon has done through using their company's high-scale systems expertise, as well as excess bandwidth and storage, in its Amazon S3 (simple storage solution) offering.

Unique Value and Marketability

Once you've determined which core competencies your company has and prioritized them by the importance of the unique value that they can offer to the marketplace, as well as your ability to defend and sustain them, the next step is to articulate the unique value the competencies offer. In doing this, you create a unique value proposition and a core strategy for engaging customers.

Core Competency	*Value Proposition*	Messaging

If you're starting from scratch, asking the right questions and targeting a yet-untapped value is the best place to begin. Next, you should build the competencies required to execute. The Google founders first asked the question, *how can we organize the data on the Web and make it easier to find?*[9] They believed answering this question would provide unique value. Yahoo and other portals didn't offer a good enough solution. It is critical to determine what value will be inherent or added to the product to engage and interact with customers, and continually pull customers back to your company.[10] This marketability shouldn't be an afterthought. And although this book will cover many ways to integrate social aspects into your marketing, integrating marketability as part of the product design is optimal.

Sometimes the technology comes first and is looking for a market. Other times it's apparent a market need isn't being met. In either case, a deep, real-time understanding of competitors, trends, and customers is required. Creating unique value requires out-of-the-box thinking and inspiration. Executives and marketers should be at the forefront of change. *Are you an early adopter of several new products each month? Do you get dozens of RSS feeds from ancillary or off-the-wall sites that can capture your imagination?*

Whether you are trying to create value with a product in development or a product on the market, there are distinct scenarios you must contend with. Let's start with the product in development. In this case, you have the opportunity to build in differentiated and engaging features or services. Marketing a product is much easier if uniqueness, social, and viral elements are built in. You can build in uniqueness by rethinking the product and approach to the market, or throw out conventional wisdom as Ryanair has done. You can segment an audience by focusing on what the market leader isn't doing, or on the needs of an untapped segment of the audience. Eons.com is the MySpace for retiring baby boomers. You can start by making your target audience part of the solution, as Digg, Craigslist, and Second Life do. And by giving your audience the freedom to forward, embed, or customize your content, you give it the potential to become viral and spread across the Web organically.

What if your product is already on the market? To steal a line from the highly successful dog behaviorist Cesar Milan, "It's never too late to rehabilitate." If your product or service is already on the market and not making the headway you expect, then focus on the fundamentals. With the viral and persuasive effects of the Live Web, product perception can be changed early or late in the game. This is where transparency and interacting come into play. If your product, service, or another behavior has failed customers in the past or failed to get attention, re-create your unique value. You can let customers inside, let them see your warts, and tell them what has changed and why. If your company has been insular in the past, make sure there are several paths customers can choose in order to affect the product. Each of us, whether we realize it or not, is willing to believe anew as long as there is a ring of truth to the story we're told, and we can experience authenticity through the company's behavior.

Once you have unique value, you must then have the tenacity, vigor, and belligerence to make it successful. In Marketing 2.0, it will be more important than ever before to get the fundamentals of marketing right. Most of us look at a runaway hit product and say to ourselves, *"How did they do it?" How did they reach a tipping point and gain extraordinary momentum?* Capturing lightning in a bottle is part accident and mostly hard work. A combination of the right people (with the needed tenacity), the right technology or solution, and the market timing line up to enable a huge, breakthrough success. But as you will see in the following examples, the successful products combine unique value with inherent marketability that engages customers and keeps them coming back. The combination creates an unstoppable virus, spreading the word beyond the early adopters.

What we learn from the huge hit is that competence, unique value, and marketability (that engages), plus focus and a good rudder, matter most. Apple's iPod was not envisioned as a stand-alone digital music player. You see, not only did the company already have the exceptional iTunes software, the team saw the flaws in the products currently available, and they had the tenacity to overcome the roadblocks.[11]

Portable MP3 players were launched in 1999, and on the market for over two years when the iPod was introduced at the end of 2001. The growth of MP3 players had been driven by the underground behavior and uprising of Napster users, who could share and download free music (which wasn't really free). Napster exploded to the tune of 50 million users, then the company imploded. The entertainment industry wasn't going to have their product given away, and anyone who wanted to download music was going to have to be tough enough to deal with the music industry's powerhouses. (In walked Steve Jobs.)

So, why has Apple enjoyed such a huge success with iPod? The product employs unique value based on the company's core competencies which is inherent in the user-friendly software, elegant hardware design, and the company's unconventional approach to solving problems. In this case, the user-friendly software is iTunes. It is well designed and unbelievably easy for just about anyone to burn CDs or download songs. Apple knew they had a great application in iTunes, and that drove the company to build the iPod. The iPod has an artistic quality and unique design that employs a wheel, which solves the problem of browsing through thousands of songs.

Notably, Apple's iPod sales didn't take off until the iTunes Music Store was launched as an integrated function of the iTunes application a year and a half after the iPod first shipped. The integrated iTunes music store (although a proprietary solution) combines all of the ingredients consumers need to make finding, purchasing, and listening to music fast, inexpensive, and fun. And the product continues to market itself *and* Apple, as users regularly come back to Apple to buy more songs, movies, and podcasts. *Remember the Sony Walkman?* You bought one, then never interacted with Sony again.

Apple's results have been impressive, and the company has built on this success by introducing dozens of variations of the product, several new services, and a mobile phone based off the iPod functions and high quality interfaces. They are taking risks, re-creating value at every turn, and transforming the media industry. Their success is due specifically to the fact that Apple entered a new market by leveraging competencies the company already had.

The iPod is more than a player and software. It is a new business process for the music industry and a magnet for Apple. Maybe only the infamously tenacious Steve Jobs could succeed with this plan. He pushed the major music establishment to agree to sell their songs online—through Apple's iTunes Music Store—reinventing the conventional music business. The paradigm shift of selling (and download-ing) one song at a time for $0.99 versus sixteen or so songs on a CD for $16.99 is more profound than it first appears. With over 1.5 billion downloads in five years, it isn't hard to believe that the one-song-per-sale paradigm could in the future far outstrip the number of songs sold grouped together via CD or online album. Tower Records has closed its doors, marking the end of one generation's cultural icon. And many news outlets are reporting that the iPod and iTunes Music Store have been a boon to musical artists and record labels, causing growth in music sales.[12]

A new approach to an existing market and engaging services also boosted Starbucks to fame and fortune. For decades, long before Star-bucks stores arrived on the scene, we happily made coffee in our homes or could get a quick cup at a nearby Dunkin' Donuts or McDonald's. Starbucks didn't invent coffee or the espresso machine. The Italian company Bezzerra was the first to manufacture espresso machines in 1901. Throughout the twentieth century, had you visited Italy or France, you would have found espresso available in cafés on almost every corner. Europeans have long gone to cafés to have a cup of coffee and socialize.

The first espresso machines arrived in the U.S. in 1927. They were mostly sold to ethnic restaurants and cafes, and it wasn't until the 1980s when "specialty coffee" became a hit in eateries across the coun-try.[13] Starbucks' first coffee bar opened in 1985. It was the early days of a trend appearing in the U.S. Starbucks' expansion to dozens of new cafes began in 1987, and by 1992, the company had opened one-hun-dred-and-sixty-five stores. Fifteen years later, there are over ten-thou-sand Starbucks locations around the world.[14]

Helped by the economic boom in the mid-1990s and Starbucks' creative coffee drinks like the Frappuccino, the company prospered. For the first time it was plausible and desirable for a wide swath of Americans to jump from paying $1.00 for a cup of coffee to over $3.00, and be quite happy doing so. But something else was happening too;

life was changing. We spent more time at our jobs, in front of our computers, and on our cellphones. Quality convenience and service became the coveted value. (Dunkin' Donuts and McDonald's have successfully served the low-end market for coffee buyers with their focus on low-cost convenience.) There are two options for customers who visit Starbucks. They can pick up a quick cup of coffee on the way to somewhere else, or they can sit completely undisturbed (by a waitress or anyone else waiting for a table) in a comfortable social environment. Friends can meet up, business people can converse with clients, and people can choose to be loud or quiet, talk on their cellphone, or work on their laptop computer. The best part is that no one expects you to order something to eat or give up your table. This was a value proposition waiting to be served.

Starbucks' unique value is behind serving *customers*, and not just coffee. Baristas get to know regular customers and interact with them. The coffee house is set up to be social, and marketing music and movies is designed to extend the social experience.[15] The deep integration of product and service is apparent in how the company makes coffee fun, tasty, and delightful. Yet, the company's size, hierarchy, and insular behavior has recently allowed for inconsistency across stores and a watered-down (less unique) atmosphere, which could become an issue. The company that innovated coffee names, coffee-cup sizes, and the ultimate coffee house community has to rethink the change in its audience's values and recreate value once again.

Unique Value and Collaboration

The Live Web unleashes the power to engage. By marshaling the functions and technology of the Live Web, companies will have an easier time creating, extending, and re-creating unique value. Without a collaborative innovation process, products will be shuttled aside by something faster, better integrated, and more interactive and delightful. We now have the tools to work with partners anywhere in the world at a much deeper level. Instead of finding the lowest-cost producer and outsourcing to them, we can co-design and co-create leveraging core competencies wherever they exist. Whether it is in product design or marketing, engaging minds and resources outside your company will give you the best opportunity to differentiate.

In a company's goal to expand and grow, often core competencies are left behind. Still, investing in what you already do well is crucial to defending your turf. By incorporating collaboration, you can look outside to help reinvigorate competencies or even establish competencies outside your core knowledge. The goal of collaboration is to turn your customers or partners into stakeholders who are invested in the company's success. In the open source software industry, there are several clear successes: Linux, Firefox, and Apache. And now we have the open source content industry, with Wikipedia and dozens of other wiki sites. In these examples, the consumers are also the developers. Either for reputation, self-interest, or reward, users get involved and own a stake in the success of the product. When consumers trust you enough to use and rely on your product for part of their core business or personal life, then they are willing to become stakeholders. This relationship works best if you let them inside and are willing to share success.

To determine where to get started on collaboration, it makes sense to evaluate the range of competencies in your company. First, you want to determine which competencies are truly *core* competencies—core to the differentiation of your business (with defendability and sustainability), and secondly, which are ancillary. The true core competencies must be protected, invested in, and grown. Everything else is up for grabs.

Do car companies need to assemble their automobiles? An automobile's customer interface has moved to the software, the brain of the car, and all of the added value that can be provided there (GPS, call for help, service updates, etc.). Assembly is a lower priority competency and uses up internal resources better focused on extending the values that draw customers to the product. The automobile makers are better off sharing the assembly IP they've garnered over the years, and collaborating with partner companies who are given a vested interest in creating greater quality in the process.

Collaboration is a new tool for all employees to learn. Products will have better definition and direction if employees collaborate and information is shared. Collaboration can extend to partners or universities where knowledge and know-how can be developed beyond corporate walls. And when it comes to creating a viral message, it often makes sense to collaborate with consumers. Companies can collaborate to extend a weak product, or to create community around an established product. Smart companies make collaboration part of the company DNA, and focus energy and resources innovating and re-innovating around a true competency.

Collaborating well with partners can become a potent core competency. There is an art to determining which projects or parts of a project must be done in-house, and which can incorporate outsiders. A successful collaboration is built on the ability to embrace outside ideas, and share information and intellectual property. Learning to be more open and using Web technologies such as RSS, wikis, and social networking features to support the process will increase success. More than just completing the project, the collaboration can produce a finished product that is better than it otherwise would have been.

Unique Value and Focus

Core Competency	Value Proposition	*Messaging*

You have determined your core competencies, and ascertained their value to your customers and in the marketplace. Now it is time to focus. You can only choose *one* value to market. This is where marketing gets difficult, *really difficult*. And this is commonly where the first mistakes are made. Your product will only be remembered for one thing *if* it gets remembered at all. But choosing just one value is risky. It means making a bet, putting all of your eggs in one basket. *What if you're wrong?* Searing focus begins when you choose one value (not two or three). Otherwise, what is developed is a list, and, well, muddy water. One differentiable value becomes your passion and creed. It is the core of your messaging and how you communicate with the outside world. You want everyone in your company to know it is the basis for what they are doing. It's better to put searing focus and exceptional execution behind the wrong bet rather than take a kaleidoscope approach with mixed execution against the right bet. With searing focus, some set of customers will be attracted to your message and remember your product. With scattered focus, no one will remember a thing. Once you choose more than one value, what you have is a list of benefits. Your competitors have the same benefits list, and your product doesn't stand out. It's not remarkable.

Searing focus requires more than choosing one value, however. You must also drive that one value across your company and deep inside each employee. A large company can remain focused if the company's leadership drives it. Each product group can maintain some level of individuality and ability to innovate too, as long as it fits under the unique value of the company. If you have searing focus on one value and drive that value throughout your company, then you have a chance that customers who need your product or want your product will find you. A clear, focused message will get through and attract an audience ready to listen.

The unique value proposition sets your product apart from your competitors. It carves out a space for your product in the marketplace, and can redefine the market and the competition.

Unique Value and Your Company DNA

In order to have a grand impact, your differentiating value must be incorporated into every part of the product and across the company.

Executives should start by institutionalizing the company or product's unique value, repeating it often and everywhere they go. The entire management team must believe in the differentiating value and stay on message, but in addition, it must be ingrained in marketing, and employees from accounting to manufacturing must be turned into believers. The apparel company Volcom establishes its edgy and youthful image through its Web site and its focus on the strong, social connections teens make through clothes, music, and art. The company's passion was born out of the behaviors and beliefs of skateboarders and has become a deep part of the company culture. Strong marketing and retailing has extended the line and their message to the general marketplace.

Each group or department in the company needs to develop the competencies that support the unique value. This will help the company sustain an advantage. Several years ago, a scalable storage systems company had identified simplicity as their unique value proposition. They had designed software that minimized or completely eliminated most storage system management tasks. (Enterprise storage is notoriously complex to manage.) When reviewing the core competencies that enabled them to offer this value proposition, they discussed how they could extend the simplicity value to the hardware with features like color-coded cables, large blinking indicator lights on the front of each storage unit, and a large LCD (display) to identify the name or serial number, which would enable fast removal of a failed storage unit without making mistakes. They also discussed customer service techniques that would enable fast identification of errors, issues with the software, or problems with storage units in a customer account. This company spent time thinking through the entire value chain for this competency. The value and concept of simple, scalable storage became the passion for the company and was driven through to all customer touchpoints.

Once you have identified what is unique, differentiable, and engaging to customers, it is time to drive the value across your company. If the value is simplicity then all elements of your business should exude this value. The value becomes your creed, for example, "We make data storage simple." The storage box is designed with simplicity as the goal—simplicity to set up, to maintain, to fix, and to uninstall the box. Service is designed with simplicity inherent too. Service is built into the product so that error messages or failures at the customer site are communicated directly to the company. The vendor could actually fix the storage box without the customer even knowing it (if they agreed to this in advance). Instead of sending in a sales rep every month to try to sell more boxes, they make sales simple by leaving several "extra" storage boxes on site at the customer's datacenter. Not only would that make sales fast, the customer could swap a new box with a broken box without any delay, making customer service extraordinary.

A software program could track all of this activity so the company knows when to charge for a new box added to the customer's network and when to apply a charge to service. Yes, accountants will find issue with leaving not-yet-paid-for goods with the customer. This does create accounting complexity. But if the accountants figure it out—competitors will be crippled.

Unique Value and Opportunity Cost

Without realizing it, marketers view the marketplace as a class system. Instead of raising the bar and creating the innovative, interesting, remarkable product, they focus on being number one. To be number one you only have to be better than the next guy in line. It's like the punch line to that old joke, *"I don't have to run faster than the bear, I just have to run faster than you."* Of course, that's only true until someone faster comes along.

To create a runaway hit, where *everyone* is chasing you, you must break out of the market-class system thinking. This is how the thinking goes. If you are in the upper class of your market you have created value, and differentiated your product. You are likely first or second in terms of market share. If you are in the middle class, you are struggling. Your product may be gaining market share but not at the speed of the upper-class players, or your product has "me too" functionality and doesn't stand on its own credibility. You haven't figured out how to separate yourself from the pack, and you have to try harder. If you are in the lower class, you are competing on price. If you don't build value into your product or service, you will spend all of your time cost-cutting and eventually lose ground as middle-class players who have some level of value lower their price and push you out.

To break out of this thinking, marketers need to look at the marketplace not just as competitors and customers, but as a clean slate or fresh opportunity. *What new approach can be used? How can you change the dynamic of the industry, as Ryanair is doing in the airline industry and Apple has done in music players? What isn't anyone else doing?* Even if you lead in your market space, it can be difficult to see what you're leaving on the table—what you could be doing to meet the needs of additional customers, or what you could do to ensure your customers don't defect and choose an alternative.

You evaluate your core competencies to determine what makes your product or service unique. Then you determine how to defend and sustain those core competencies through constant innovation. Throughout this process you must keep asking, *does the product engage and delight customers?* A loyalty program that enables customers to earn points and get something for free often delights. However, it's not defensible; it's something any competitor can easily implement. iPod, iTunes, and the iTunes Music Store delight customers, and they are sticky because they are engaging. Customers get involved and keep coming back. In fact, the solution delights customers so much that the proprietary nature of the product doesn't hold back sales.

If your strategy simply isn't working, it may be time to throw off the blinders and rethink what you are doing. You know what your core competencies are and you have your product. Determine if the core of the product can be used in a completely different way for a new market or segment. Reinventing what you have been doing can feel as though you are throwing away all of your work. Yet it makes great sense to leverage what you have that works and throw away what isn't working, especially if you can be substantially more successful targeting a different audience (possibly untapped) in another market.

The work you do to determine your core competencies helps to illuminate what is unique and what is differentiable about your product, and what you can defend, sustain, and delight customers with.

4 | VOICE

IN AN INTERACTIVE, SOCIAL MARKETPLACE, VOICE HAS LEGS.

Voice is a communications platform—a chosen value system, passion, and personality. Your company voice is inherent in your marketing materials, videos, ads, and Web pages. Voice can have such a strong connection with your audience that they walk and talk your value on your behalf, providing reach you may not be able to attain on your own. Your company's voice is defined through the narrative you create, and that narrative encompasses your company style, tone, view of the marketplace, vision of the future, and passion. It is what the company becomes through its statements and behaviors in the eyes of its customers and the marketplace.

Everyone knows GoDaddy is irreverent, and Apple is cool. It may at first appear that this is simply corporate image developed through advertising. But rather, the image of each of these companies is a finely crafted and defined voice, established through executives, employees, communications, and marketing. Authenticity and consistency make your specific voice ring true to your audience. (And a much bigger discussion on authenticity follows in the next chapter.) It is a believable voice that makes it clear to the marketplace what can be expected of your company, enabling positive, interesting, and valuable interactions.

There are three forms of voice: *inform, connect*, and *engage*. Your marketing can deploy any of these, or all three. When you inform your audience, you create an understanding of product, company, market, competitors, or customers. To connect with your audience, you develop an approachable platform and message, often executed through a character or story which offers some type of emotional appeal. Yet to create relevance with your audience—and it's relevance that pulls them in—you engage them with a compelling message of why the company (or product) exists, and how it will change people's lives. This vision and passion compels your audience to partake in your journey.

Often the choice of voice used by a company is an unconscious decision; it evolves with the company and its values. In this Live Web where content and message are easily separated from brand, it is imperative you shape and establish a strategic voice to rise above the chaos. How you define your voice—your *tone, style*, and *personality*—determines who will hear your message, believe your message, and follow. Not only do you want to find an original voice, you need to describe an enticing journey and destination (a *vision*) so that others will choose to join you. And to do that, you have to be clear about the scope and direction of your business.

Addressing business vision, the highly regarded Harvard Business School professor Theodore Levitt in the 1960s challenged railroad executives with the question "What business are you in?" He pushed them to see that they weren't in the *railroad* business; they were in the *transportation* business.[1] Levitt painted a picture that opened up new opportunities. Google could define their market as search, but the company's *vision* is to organize the world's information and make it accessible. Apple could define their markets as computers and consumer electronics, but they clearly see their opportunity as the entertainment business. McNeil PPC, Inc., the maker of Tylenol, states their purpose is *to become the largest U.S. consumer healthcare company*. Becoming the number one company by any metric is not a vision. Yet, you will find hundreds, if not thousands of companies that state leadership as their only mission, vision, purpose, or goal. The message of leadership doesn't inform, connect, or engage.

Communicate to Inform

We inform our audience in a number of ways. We state that our drug is clinically proven to stop erectile dysfunction, or that our claim is backed up by statistics such as one in five adults suffers from headache or migraine, or that one in one-hundred-and-fifty children in the U.S. will be diagnosed with autism. Web sites often state in a matter of fact manner the product's performance statistics, or features and functions. We often read bravado such as "the world's fastest," "the cheapest available," or "the safest choice." Without the facts and figures to back up these statements, they are nothing more than hot air, and they serve to diminish real value. Often facts get lost in the clutter, too many companies saying the same thing.

Sometimes facts are illustrated better in a video. And now that online video is easily shared, it can be the ambassador for a company's brand and voice. Blendtec has enjoyed great success with this approach on their WillItBlend.com site. Where the company could have chosen to state, "Our blender is more powerful than any other," they instead produced a cadre of videos of a man "blending" a golf club, a handful of cellphones, a rake, forty pens, and cassette tapes among many other items.[2] (Warning, if you watch the videos, you'll want to buy the blender.) Facts can help substantiate your message, but alone they are flat, static pieces of data that do nothing to connect or engage.

Video can replace volumes of text or technical data. While informative, video can be humorous, provocative, and a more coherent platform to make your point. Monsanto Co. filmed testimonials from farmers around the world to make a case for bioengineered crops. The company posted the clips on their Web site (under biotech) attracting more than fifteen-thousand visitors a month. Getting past the technical jargon, videos tell a compelling story. Wal-Mart, General Motors

Corp., and Coldwell Banker all use video on their Web sites to communicate with internal and external audiences.[3] Video is a standard tool of the Live Web. In fact, video is so powerful it launched the YouTube juggernaut and dozens of Web TV sites. Live Web audiences simply love their video. With third-party content delivery networks such as Akamai Technologies Inc. and Limelight Inc., any Web site can provide video streaming with excellent performance.

Analogies marshal a stronger emotional reaction than plain facts. Blendtec videos are a type of analogy. If it will blend a rake, it will most certainly blend ice. A potent use of analogy is illustrated by Trocaire.org in their gender inequality public service announcement. The ad states that the babies shown (in the video) have been born with something that affects more people than malaria, cancer, HIV, or AIDS. *They were born female in a third world country and killed or victimized by discrimination, neglect, or abuse.* The analogy works. Even though we may already be aware that young girls and infants are mutilated, or in some countries killed at birth for being born female, we likely didn't know the problem was as big as some of the worst diseases plaguing our planet.

Analogies and metaphors are tools marketers have used for years. Beyond an advertisement, they are a great way to communicate online. Analogies are quotable for the press and bloggers. They enable your audience to connect with your message. Analogies take facts and help us relate to them. Relating to your audience is the first step to making a connection and getting someone to act.

Communicate to Connect

Marketing messages that are aligned with the company voice, unexpected, and offer emotional appeal together create a strong connection with audiences. In the "Impossible is Nothing" David Beckham Adidas commercial (sixty-second spot on YouTube), the statement made by Beckham is personal and revealing. It's not just that Beckham overcame his mistakes and weaknesses to reap extraordinary success. It is his willingness to open up to the audience and reveal his innermost feelings in an unexpected format. As consumers, we are more likely to remember something unexpected. Adidas is a believable sponsor because the company consistently positions itself as being about you and where you are going in life, not just sports and athletes. The message is aligned with Adidas' voice.

Adidas has carried through with the personal expression approach in their marketing via other campaigns. In the company's Adicolor campaign, they put up a white billboard with only their logo, and placed the billboard on walls where people would likely paint on it.[4] It wasn't long before the billboards were covered with graffiti. Adidas papered over the graffiti with a new billboard sheet of an Adidas tennis shoe, but allowed some of the graffiti to show through as the design of the shoe. In 2006, Adidas launched "Paint Your Own Sneakers" with a limited edition kit that included 1983-style, all-white sneakers and color kits so that consumers could produce their own look. Adidas has found a way to connect and interact with their audience and offer relevance. They have built a marketing platform—a voice that is engaging.

HP's 2006 Fingerskilz.tv campaign, however, missed the mark. The company produced a blog, and uploaded videos they hoped would become viral. And with one-hundred-and-eighty-thousand unique visitors, they had good success *for the viral goal*.[5] The homemade-looking videos feature the antics of finger footballers (fingers painted as soccer players). The campaign was kicked off during World Cup Soccer, and designed to rise above the din of the marketing tornado this sporting event draws. At the end of the campaign, it was revealed that HP was behind Fingerskilz.

The problem is that the hip or cool factor doesn't fit HP. There's nothing cool about the company, not in the look or feel of its PCs or laptops, not in the Web site, logo or executive personalities. Apple is cool. HP is not. So, although the campaign drew interest, it didn't connect the brand with viewers, or offer relevance. And worse, it lacked authenticity. Doing viral marketing for the sake of a video becoming viral is a waste of time and energy. You will connect with your audience when your marketing fits the voice, vision, positioning, and story of the company.

Communicate to Engage

Every time you communicate with your target audience you are attempting to engage them with your voice. To engage audiences, the core of your voice must be your passion or creed, your vision of the future, or your desire to create change. Your voice can illustrate your view of the world or the marketplace, contain purpose, and inspire through your beliefs, but to be believable, it must align with how your company behaves.

The outdoor clothing and gear company Patagonia has combined its vision and philosophy for the company with its creed to be environmentally responsible (and to get others to be, too). The company has strong standards for quality in its products and defines its quality metrics in detail (functionality, multifunctionality, durability, customer fit, simplicity, easy to care for, artistic, authentic, innovative, global design, and value add) so that employees understand the rules under which they can create.[6] Further, the company continuously finds ways to incorporate reusable materials in order to reduce the negative impact on the environment. Of course a clean, healthy environment furthers the prospects of the company, since they can only sell to outdoor enthusiasts if there is an outdoors worth going to.

Patagonia's voice is consistent and strong across the company's Web site, blog, catalog, advertisements, and all other marketing materials and communications. The company doesn't clutter or confuse its message of quality products with minimal environmental impact targeted to its core customer—rock climber, surfer, skier, and snowboarder. Patagonia's management and employees exude outdoor enthusiasm, and employees can comfortably speak to the company vision.

Apple's voice communicates creativity, design quality, and entertainment with everything the company does and says. The company lives its voice and vision much like Patagonia. Macs, MacBooks, iPods, iTunes, and the iTunes Music Store all combine unique features with elegant design and extraordinary ease of use. The passion goes beyond products. Steve Jobs practices his presentations for hours in advance until they are as good as a Broadway play, so that his performance extends the company's "wow" factor. From the early stages of the company, unique design has been Apple's hallmark for cool. Apple has consistently offered products to the ordinary person who wants to stand out.

The company has found a brilliant form for telling their story in the "Get a Mac" ads, where two humans represent a PC and a Mac. (You can find these on ifilm.com or YouTube.) As they speak to each other, it is apparent the Mac is smart, savvy, and interesting. The PC is clueless. And although the ads state the obvious (if you've ever used a Mac and a PC), the story is clever and offered in an unexpected format, so it pulls us in. But more than that, it is clearly aligned with Apple's view of the marketplace, vision, and voice.

Amazon has taken advantage of video and entertainment elements of the Live Web with its branded online channel Amazon Fishbowl and host Bill Maher. By interviewing famous authors, or celebrities who have written a book, or featuring musical artists who have recently released a new CD, Amazon has strategically brought its products to life, and extended its vision of the marketplace. Not only has the Web channel attracted big-name sponsors minimizing Amazon's cost, Fishbowl specifically markets the products Amazon sells. The show quality, product focus, and branding Amazon has deployed through Fishbowl successfully extends the company vision and message. Amazon is more than a product warehouse, they are a customer-needs fulfillment service.

What happens when your message is not believable? Consider how much play in the press Google's internal motto, "Do No Evil" has gotten. When a company grows to thousands of employees, works in dozens of countries and has billions in the bank, it is likely to do some evil at some point in time—just ask ex-employees, or small Web companies ousted off the top-of-page organic search results when Google updates its algorithms. Because Google wields so much power due to its dominant market share and financial strength, "Do No Evil" doesn't ring authentic with much of its audience. And although an internal message targeted to employees to guide their behavior, the motto is used publicly by the company to separate itself from, and make a jab at Microsoft, commonly known in Silicon Valley circles as the Evil Empire.

A more subtle interpretation of the believability problem is illustrated in the Robert Baggio for Johnnie Walker commercial. A well-known football (a.k.a. soccer) player like Beckham, Baggio misses a penalty kick in the World Cup Soccer match and has to live with his mistake for four years. Then he is able to redeem himself during the next World Cup Soccer tournament by making a penalty kick. Although sports fans can relate to his humiliation and frustration with his team (and country) losing the match because he didn't make the kick, the story feels contrived. What we expect to happen does happen, so the message fades into the background of our over-marketed-to brains. The execution of the ad lacks the unexpected devices used to tell the Beckham for Adidas story. Connection and relevance are missing. Even though the ad is consistent with the voice projected by the company, and their strategy to integrate brand and logo into a consistent message of personal progress and personal journey, the company would strengthen its story by using the real people stories collected on their Web site, which offer depth and greater relevance to the rest of their audience.

Giving your product a story, or life beyond its functions, is especially engaging for today's consumers. Dole Organic helps consumers learn about and experience the origin and life behind its fruit. Consumers can go to Dole Organic's Web site and type in a three-digit code found on the fruit sticker, and view photos of crops and local workers, and access additional background information.[7] The Live Web is driving a more educated consumer to demand more transparency from companies. Providing transparency through story is both engaging and informative.

The best part of forming your platform for voice is that it makes you think through all of the elements of your strategy, and how they fit into your vision. You know when people believe what you are saying. They are nodding their heads, asking questions, and interacting. People will actually ask you how they can become a part of your journey. However, not everybody reacts positively to the voice they hear from a company. There are people who believe what you say and want to join in, people who disagree with you, and people who aren't listening.

The people who aren't listening don't associate with your vision, passion, and creed, or don't believe you. The people who argue with you have a vested interest somewhere else. Segmenting your audience in this way (just for the purpose of this exercise) can help focus your marketing activities. You can choose to ignore or respond to the nay-sayers (depending on who they are), but you don't want to focus you marketing or your energy on them. Your focus is on *your* voice, *your* positioning, and *your* message. The goal is to find new and inventive ways to substantiate your voice and your message. This verification process will be covered in detail in Chapter Five.

Analyzing and evaluating your audience drives you to take charge of what you communicate. There are always more examples you can add, new analogies, and unique formats to illustrate your voice, and gather more followers. Better yet, you can invite your audience to tell the message for you, and in their own words. The ability to engage your audience in this way empowers your message.

The Elements of Voice

Voice is meant to connect with your audience and offer relevance. To do that, voice requires several elements: *image, vision,* and *positioning.* When you get started defining your voice, ask yourself these questions: *Why does this company exist? What image or personality has it formed or is it trying to form? What is the company point-of-view in terms of the product, the market, and the world? Where is the industry going? Where is the company going? Where is it taking customers?*

Image

Image isn't just for Hollywood celebrities and luxury automobiles. Your customers have a perception of your company (right or wrong), and each move the company makes helps to define that image (whether planned or unplanned). Making choices that support and illustrate the image you want the company to have is the key to managing customer perceptions. First you have to know what image you want the company to project. *Is the company visionary, creative, cool, edgy, pragmatic, safe, for the price-sensitive, for the masses, or for the elite?*

Managing your image is a daily activity. If you don't want an image as a high-flying, arrogant, self-centered company, then treat all of your employees with respect (even the ones you don't like), and ensure you are treating all of your customers with care (even the small ones). Silicon Valley start-ups which often begin with a passion and a purpose, regularly become infamous for forgetting these rules as soon as they hit the big time.

Image is created by the choices made across the company, not by advertising agencies through the advertising campaigns they create. Image is in the product, the employees, the Web site, the business processes, the partnerships, and the marketing. When you define your image, the next step is to ensure the choices made across the company support and enhance that image. If you choose not to define your image, your customers, competitors, or partners will likely do it for you. *Who would you rather put in charge?*

Vision

You don't have to develop an image as a visionary to express a vision for your company, products, or industry. *Vision* is the ability to define business, product, industry trends, or the future in terms of customers or the marketplace, before they have taken shape. Further, it is easier for customers to follow you, if you give them some sense that you know where you and your industry are going. There is also a much stronger trust between the company and the customer, if the customer believes you are the company that can take them forward. Many people feel vision is reserved for high technology companies who have to show that they understand industry trends, have deep technical chops, and can take their products forward, leapfrogging the competition in performance, price, or functionality—or all three. Vision is about more than technology.

Does a clothing retailer have to have a vision? What about a high-performance cooking equipment company? Ask Volcom or Viking. Each of these companies shows passion towards the industry they're in, towards the technology or resources they incorporate, and towards the future. Their vision keeps customers coming back for more.

Volcom's creed is "youth against establishment" which appeals to its core skateboarder and snowboarder audience. It easily extends itself to any teen with a social conscious, or that gets pissed-off at their parents every now and then. Volcom's strategy to find or create what defines edgy, individual, and anti-establishment through music, art, videos, movies, and athletes, draws their audience forward with them, even while they sell their clothes through the dominant established retailers including Nordstroms, Macy's, and Chicks sporting goods.

For Viking, kitchens are a passion. Although all of the top-tier, high-performance kitchen equipment companies provide exceptional products (which you would expect at that price), only Viking defines a vision of cooking and living with their products. Viking creates the image of its stovetops, ranges, refrigerators, barbecues, and dishwashers as lifestyle products. The company expresses its vision by continually investing in the lifestyle of cooking which includes recipes, cooking classes, and travel to great food destinations. Customers know they will learn more, get better service, and always have new choices with Viking.

Positioning

Your image and vision define your company and its position in the industry in which you work, and relative to competitors or alternatives. Positioning has an even more influential role. It allows you to define the market on *your* terms. There are several paths you can take to define the market on your terms. You can name the market by creating a new term (personal digital assistant), or segment the market to create a new niche (nighttime medicine). You can reposition your competitors, defining their offering more narrowly. You can pour so much focus and passion on your differentiating value that it appears there are no competitors in your space, or that your competitors will be unable to catch up. If you choose not to define the market on your terms, then you are forced to work within some other company's framework. The market will see you as a follower. It will be difficult to break out and be heard, and even more difficult to lead with an intriguing voice and vision.

By the mid-1990s, Sun Microsystems' storage division had long been a follower. It trailed far behind EMC, the leader in (big box) enterprise storage. To gain an edge, Sun chose to develop the anti-EMC strategy: stack up lots of small storage boxes, manage them with software, and make them act like a big enterprise storage system. The value in this strategy was flexibility and lower cost. (In reality, it created greater complexity and higher management costs in the short-term).

Each time Sun visited an enterprise customer that used EMC, the Sun sales reps and marketers were forced to hear a litany of reasons why the customer loved EMC. But Sun quickly figured out that EMC's strengths were also its weaknesses—and Sun pounced on them. At a time when data centers were moving to storage area networks (SANs), small and manageable sounded good. Sun repositioned EMC as the expensive, closed, proprietary, BIG box. You had to call EMC, then wait for them to send a technical support person out to your site just to replace a disk! They even lock their storage box with a proprietary screwdriver to make sure you, the customer, can't get in. Now, this you could have fun with. Repositioning the industry leader as closed, difficult, and inflexible had an impact on customers' perceptions, and Sun storage sales increased because of the position they took.[8]

We often see how a company's passion and the position they take in the market seeps into every element of marketing. The passion for the outdoors, for great entertainment, or for universally accessible information sets the stage for the company's voice. It repositions the trends in the marketplace to fit the company's worldview. It defines the market on the marketer's terms.

The Power of Story

Story is an engaging platform for a company's voice. A great story takes the audience on a journey. The audience plays a part, and becomes involved. One of the best examples of story used as a marketing vehicle is the Jared Fogle ads for Subway. Originally, Subway had launched a campaign touting the health of its sandwiches by stating the fact that seven sandwiches had six grams of fat. The campaign had little impact on audience behavior. Then a student at Indiana University, weighing in at four-hundred-and-twenty-five pounds, decided to put himself on a Subway sandwich diet. (Okay, the six grams of fat marketing campaign peaked at least Fogle's interest.) And with a little exercise and Subway sandwiches, Jared Fogle lost two-hundred-and-forty-five pounds. Subway launched the story in ads, and extended it through their Web site, national press, and tours across the United States, keeping Fogle as their spokesperson. By using Jared Fogle's story and personality, Subway went from being just another fast food restaurant, to a company with an effective platform—they help people lose weight.

Starbucks has taken a different path with story. The company has completely remade the coffee paradigm, mimicking the value-add positioning used in the wine business. Wines get their names and value from the region of origin, the vineyard, and the grapes used. Leveraging this approach, Starbucks has created a story around coffee bean regions, bean growers, and bean names.[9] The regional story adds dimension and perceived value, so customers aren't surprised by the high price.

A Failure to Engage

The naked truth is that *you no longer have absolute control over your brand and marketing.* You can be an influential force on the market, but the traditional top-down, push approach falls flat. How you approach the market requires change. Simply positioning your brand and pushing out a message is no longer going to work. Engage your audience. Start a conversation. Interact. It is time to become a part of what is happening on the Net, and to create a passionate and interesting place for visitors to experience. That is what Nike has done with their social site Joga.com (in a joint program with Google) and with their NikeSoccer.com *365 Todays* online magazine (ezine).

The music and broadcast industries are prime examples of what happens when you drag your feet, ignoring sweeping changes across your industry and on the Internet. It was the late 1990s when Wink Communications, the first company to provide interactive TV, began courting TV networks and cable companies. Wink made it possible for viewers to interact with TV programming, and even purchase products while watching a commercial. Tivo and other digital video recorders (DVRs), which enable consumers to automatically record and playback television shows at their convenience, were shunned by the broadcast giants, mostly because they made it possible for viewers to pass over commercials—TV's main revenue stream. The Wink and Tivo technology for interactive television would have enabled the networks to beat Internet companies to the punch when it came to tying ad revenue to information and entertainment, but it was summarily rejected.

Only in the past few years have cable companies finally gotten around to incorporating Tivo-style digital video recorder (DVR) functionality into their set-top boxes. With this added value they can use the technology to promote and enhance their services and add new services.

The TV networks now have to rely on the cable companies or Tivo for this functionality, and are only slowly learning how to leverage these partners to better market their assets. They are far behind the curve.

And if that isn't bad enough, prime-time television shows have been hijacked by users uploading them to MySpace and YouTube. The major media companies are losing control over their brand and their audience as Web distribution changes the rules. TV shows and movies are now available to stream or download from Web channels which include the iTunes Music Store, Yahoo!TV, MSN Primetime, AOL In2TV, Amazon Unbox, and so many others. The networks and cable companies may own the content, but they can't figure out how to empower their brand and their vision through this new channel—yet.

There is a similar story in the music industry. A decade ago, computer companies entering or growing their media-server businesses were imploring music companies to digitize and market their huge music catalogs and put them online.[10] Content was going digital, and either the major players could lead the charge or drag their feet. The ideas—and warning over what was to come—fell on deaf ears. Napster had driven the craze for digitizing then sharing music online (illegally) to the tune of 50 million users. The trend was obvious and instead of adopting a strategy to compete, and incorporating a vision of how music will be purchased, shared, and delivered in the future, music companies including Universal Music Group (UMG) chose to fight Napster through legal channels only. They won the battle, but lost the war.

While the music industry stuck its proverbial head in the sand, the Web has driven forward. Today, music is shared or sold via Apple's iTunes Music Store, Real Networks' Rhapsody site, MySpace, Yahoo!, YouTube, Amazon, and others. It appears UMG has lost its passion for music and its vision for the industry. The company continues to focus most of its energy on legal avenues to stop competition. Its latest battle is with MySpace, a social Web site where users upload content, some of which is copyrighted. Content companies have the right to protect their content just as other companies have the right to protect their patents. However, the entertainment industry is figuring out that it is better to "coopetate" (compete and cooperate) than to endlessly sue to gain control.[11] The Internet creates complexity and chaos beyond what most companies are used to, and control is a thing of the past. Learning how to market, collaborate, and integrate in this new age can mean the difference between success and failure.

The music industry has left the door open to companies like Sellaband (www.sellaband.com) which takes advantage of the Live Web to provide a new take on the music business. The service makes it possible for new musical artists to attract fans who are willing to invest in their band to help them cut a CD. The grassroots audience behavior can propel the band into stardom, and a deal with a record label. The process ensures word-of-mouth since the investors (fans) have a vested interest in seeing the band take off. UMG, Sony BMG, or any other music company could have introduced this concept along with first rights to represent the artist if the band garnered a strong audience following.

While the big league content companies have been dragged into the digital age kicking and screaming, the digerati and consumers have taken the helm and are driving the vision, the direction, the message, the medium, and the money. There is no better example of market failure due to companies that stopped creating the vision of the future. It is clear their lack of execution weakened the power of their voice.

The premiere content owners, including NBC Universal, Time Warner Entertainment, Sony BMG Music, Universal Music Group, The Walt Disney Company (ABC), CBS Corporation, Fox Broadcasting, and others have lost their image as the kings of media. They are not defining the vision, the future, or the value in the industry they once owned. Yet in 2007, they started seriously investing in the Live Web. Many of these companies now syndicate content, collaborate to manage and distribute their content, and are beefing up their Web sites to attract viewers.[12] They are trying to overcome the less than satisfying deals they have been forced to commit to with the Internet elite.

Smart companies develop a strong vision and an authentic voice. They continually adjust and adapt as the world around them changes, and strengthen their voice with more truths that prove it out. In this new age of marketing where anyone can set up a Web site and compete with you, or set up a blog and communicate about you, lacking execution against your strategy and vision will almost certainly cause you to lose the power of your voice—and your position in the market, or you'll simply never gain one in the first place.

An Authentic Voice

For your voice to become authentic, you must use it to infect the DNA of your company. Every employee should be able to communicate the company's tone, style, and personality, as well as the vision, in their own words. Your customers should be able to breathe your words as if they are employed by you. Let us consider in more detail how Viking Range Corporation sells lifestyle over cooking products.

One would think the professional styling and features of Viking products would attract a narrow market of home chefs. Yet, many people who own them don't cook much or all that well. Viking doesn't try to make you believe their stovetop or oven will turn you into a chef. That wouldn't be authentic. What Viking believes, and what they want you to believe, is that if you own Viking products, you live well, travel extensively, and know good wine, good food, and good people. And if you don't, you soon will. Viking extends their position and platform with cooking schools and cooking trips to exotic places. If you own Viking, when guests arrive, you show off the kitchen first (and you even love talking about your range). Viking has figured out how to connect with its audience in a meaningful way. Customers want to go on the Viking journey. Viking has seeped their values throughout the company and onto their Web site—while competitors Thermador and Wolf communicate only technology and product.

When Larry Page and Sergey Brin developed Google search, they simply wanted to make it easier to find stuff on the Internet. Today, the company vision is about organizing the world's information and making it universally accessible and useful. Since that includes music, television programming, movies, user-generated content, news, and books, among other forms of information, Google has morphed into a media conglomerate. And each time Google inks a deal with a content provider or a media business with millions of viewers, listeners, or users, the company adds one more plot to the storyline, and audiences believe they will succeed along their journey. When they do something that appears contrary to their stated vision, consumers scratch their heads and wonder what Google is really up to, that is, until the company helps us see how it fits in their plans.

An authentic voice is backed up by all the company does and says. Customers believe in the behavior they see over the words that they hear. Whether you are marketing crystal glasses for wine drinkers or laptop computers for business travelers, your voice communicated effectively will drive customers to choose your product over another. The most important elements of a believable voice are passion and execution. You must drive the product to be everything you envision.

Make it a Real Conversation

It's a conversation, but it's not the same kitchen-table chatter of yore. In the modern age of marketing, external communications—one of the key opportunities to express your voice—has never before been held in such high esteem. Web-based business owners and Fortune 1000 companies alike are finding that they can reap huge benefit from online press, article marketing, and blogging—for some, enough benefit to delay or replace advertising.

A blog is the essential conversation starter. To blog is to be part of the Live Web. Savvy companies do it right, enabling readers to leave comments, and adding tags so that the conversation and company become part of the bigger conversations in the Webosphere. You can take advantage of online news aggregators such as Techmeme, Magit, and Digg by incorporating buttons for quick linking of your articles to these sites, or by posting articles on hotly-debated current topics other bloggers are talking about. *Looking for stuff to talk about on your blog?* Click on over to Technorati, Alexa, or Blogpulse and see what other bloggers are focused on.

Blogs give you and your employees a personal voice. They are real-time unlike Web sites, brochures, or press releases. Major news media read blogs. They get ideas, and they get to know corporate executives better. Blogs are an incredible environment to hear what your readers think, and to learn who is interested in linking to you. They provide a natural place to position yourself and company as the knowledge center on any subject, the first place to go to learn something new, and the ability to link out to what others might be saying or doing.

Patagonia started their blog, The Cleanest Line, in early 2007. It carries on their message of environmental advocacy. It positions the company at the forefront of this issue. But more importantly, it opens up a conversation with employees and customers. It also gives a voice to their biggest advocates offering relevancy and information to a broader audience. Sun Microsystems has gotten huge kudos for the blog from CEO Jonathan Schwartz. Highly regarded as the first CEO blogger, Jonathan has helped set a new tone for the company, a more open and interactive tone.

As consumers take control over what ads they will allow into their homes, onto their PCs, or cellphones, public relations (PR) can be an effective means for getting your message heard. Turning your message into news, trends, or insights can gain coverage from extensive online outlets. With enough interest, the message is distributed and linked to across the Web organically. (It's pulled rather than pushed.) Business publications, trade publications, and newspapers have online editions that give us instantaneous news and information. Key industry influencers and bloggers provide daily insights that can be accessed by a broad audience. There are myriad opportunities to influence, relate, and communicate your view, vision, and voice.

The real-time nature of information on the Web, as well as the profusion of information, has changed the effects of a good PR campaign. There are hundreds or thousands more venues to communicate. With many people adopting RSS readers (automatically receiving news on their desktop, laptop, or mobile phone) or aggregating their own news preferences on their Yahoo! or Google homepages, news is much more accessible. Consumers view news in real-time from hundreds of sources and can receive your message from a variety of sources they trust. Communicating your message through bloggers, news publications, or trade magazines online is simply effective.

Becoming the expert and source for your industry can be accomplished by offering deep, useful information—free. The goal is to create an environment where everyone comes to your Web site first. That requires developing fresh, in-depth materials and posting them often, and offering a social experience where interesting people are talking. It also means linking out to other useful resources. Once again, it's about being porous, recognizing it's not all about you, but that to find out what it is all about, people will want to come to your place of business.

Extending this platform, you can push out useful information through article marketing. The process of writing an article with your byline about anything in your industry (while allowing your point-of-view to permeate it), and placing it with an appropriate Web site can draw hundreds or thousands of eyeballs to your Web site. And anyone can do it. With so many publications and bloggers online competing to write unique and compelling stories, they are always looking for good material—so, be an asset, be informative. You don't want to ignore bloggers as an outlet for your message. You will attract them by being quotable (pithy) and open to interviews with smaller blog sites. (If their work is good, they will develop a large following.)

You can add a blog to your Web site using Wordpress or Movable Type software, or quickly set up a blog on Wordpress.com, Blogger.

com, or Typepad.com. All you need is a point-of-view and something to say. Being informative, interesting, fascinating, or simply educational, a blog can substantiate your company's view of the world, and establish why customers should be in your camp. Although a blog should be written by a person who embodies the passion and drive behind the company to ensure it is authentic, PR firms can help you market your blog and capture a broad audience of readers.

A blog can also pull potential customers to your business, and change how you interact with them. Stormhoek Winery, Northfield Construction, 800-CEO-READ, and Aldo Coffee Co. are all small companies that blog. In a marketing campaign targeted only to bloggers, Stormhoek shipped a free bottle of wine to bloggers in specific geographic regions in order to entice them to write about the company. It worked. The broader conversation impacted the approach the vineyard used with resellers and consumers and has had a significant impact on these relationships, and wine sales doubled in less than twelve months.[13] Stormhoek continues the atmosphere of listening, learning, and interacting with their audiences in a personal and inviting company blog.

Not many construction companies blog and most people don't know much about the construction company they hire. Northfield Construction has broadened their audience, and become an integrated member of their local community by revealing the company's daily activities, and discussing events that affect the community on their blog. 800-CEO-READ's Daily Blog does a good job of offering snippets to its busy target audience of CEOs who like to read. And as you might expect, Aldo Coffee creates a personal relationship with customers by making the company transparent—helping them to stand out from Starbucks.[14]

What do all of these blogs have in common? They give their audience a sense of who the people are behind the company, what matters to them, as well as a sense of openness and transparency, and the opportunity for customers to interact. They have all successfully made the conversation real and ongoing, and established their own voice.

Embrace the Voices Within

Employees are a company's best agents for disseminating and strengthening the product message, and company voice. Today this valuable resource can be deployed in the marketplace. IBM has thousands of employee bloggers. They post their personal opinions, personal information, technical, and business expertise, and even unsupported IBM product configurations. You can get a list of many of these blogs at www.ibm.com/blogs. There's some incredibly useful information: Jean-François Arseneault's *Life in Technical Sales*, Michael Dolan's *Linux, Law, Open Source, and a Comedy of Errors*, and Jeff Jonas', *A Collection of Thoughts and Resources on Privacy and the Information Age* to name a few. It takes a trusting management team to empower the voices of its employees. Microsoft also has thousands of bloggers. Robert Scoble, now an ex-Microsoft employee, is one of the most well-known. His technical depth and informative posts have given some transparency to a company that traditionally has been insular.

Jonathan Schwartz took his passion for open dialogue a step further by opening up blogging to all Sun Microsystems employees. To ensure employees know what the rules are, the company publicly posts its blogging guidelines and policy on public discourse.[15] Google, Yahoo, HP, and others enable employee blogging. You might expect technology companies to widely adopt blogging and other social media, but all types of companies are opening up internally and externally, including Boeing, Stoneyfield Farm, GM, Ford, Forrester Research, NYSE, Park City Mountain Resort, Patagonia, Sprint, Telstra, Walker Art Center, Wells Fargo, Merrill Lynch, Disney, Motorola, Raytheon, McGraw-Hill, and Starbucks.

There are far too many executives that will not consider allowing employees to post blogs or their personal and professional information. Management wants command and control even though they can see the Live Web is eroding this position. The vast opportunity offered by the Live Web is lost on these executives. Becoming more open, authentic, and interactive will change how a company behaves both internally and externally. It can redefine processes for product development and outbound marketing.

Blogs have evolved quickly in the past few years. Although they began as a simple-to-create web page that enabled any single person to write their personal thoughts or opinions, they have quickly evolved to corporate communications platforms. A blog can be used to educate; it can be used to illustrate; and it can be used to market your message (although, hopefully in a subtle manner). To pull customers and prospects in closer, companies set up a blog and engage in a conversation. Blogging allows for anyone who reads the blog to comment on it, tag a post (article), and even vote on the best one (if you offer that feature). Audiences view companies that blog as being more open and accessible. Executives or employees get to say what they think, and customers can respond. *Could there be a more engaging or easier exchange of ideas?*

5

VERIFIABLE

TRUST IS MORE IMPORTANT THAN GREAT PRODUCTS.

Verification in one form is completely straight-forward. It is about providing the proof to back up your statements and assertions as true. Proof can be in the ability to measure your unique value proposition, making it much more persuasive. And, it can be in the form of a product demo, or customer case history, proving out the functionality and performance of your product. On the other hand, how customers verify through their personal "truth meter" if a company is authentic and believable, is a little more nebulous, and requires more thoughtful analysis. *Verification* is in the data, facts, demos, white papers, and so much more. But at its core, verification is about building trust and gaining credibility—a company's most valued assets.

All forms of verification can lead to customer trust, and when customers trust your product and your company, their loyalty and advocacy rise to the surface. Even great products—leaders of their industry—suffer a terrible backlash when trust is broken, just ask Intel, Sun Microsystems, Kryptonite, McNeil PPC, Inc., and RC2 Corp. (makers of Thomas & Friends train toys). These companies chose to cover up or minimize serious product issues, or were faced with a critical product issue that could have been avoided. Often, this can be a result of top-down, corporate-culture problems where management isn't exhibiting open or authentic behaviors. And you can be sure, if customers can't trust your company, they will purchase somewhere else, sooner or later.

There are many ways to build trust with your audience, and this needs to be taken as seriously as product design and innovation. You start building trust by framing your market position, vision, passion, and creed in a narrative that customers learn from, relate to, and connect with as discussed in the previous chapter. Every interaction prospects or customers have with your company must fit with the narrative and style you have chosen. Each of these interactions and touchpoints also act as points of verification—when they are consistent.

As consumers, we have become better informed about marketing spin, and have a deeper sense for when we are being told the truth, and when we are being manipulated. In fact, we tend to be a bit cynical when it comes to marketing messages. And we should be, since we are constantly reminded that marketers are willing to manipulate. Even so, we can still be fooled—at least for a brief moment—as illustrated in the following examples.

In March 2007, Nissan scattered twenty-thousand car keys in night clubs and hot spots around the U.S. with a note that read, "If found, please do not return. My Next Generation Nissan Altima has Intelligent Key with Push Button Ignition, and I no longer need these."[1] So, you have interrupted your evening to do the right thing and bend down to pick up the keys, only to find you've been duped. Maybe the ruse will go viral. Maybe it will be one more reason why Americans don't trust advertisers.

Some marketers invade our homes with their tricks. With concern, you open an envelope marked *financial information inside, open immediately*" only to find a pitch to refinance your mortgage. When your credit-card company calls during dinner, you take a moment to listen because it could be important. Yet, it is a telemarketer selling more services. Worse, when you read a blog, you can no longer be sure the voice is authentic. Sadly, Wal-Mart, Sony, and others have broken that trust too by paying people to blog their message, as if it is coming from a real customer.[2] Blogging was pioneered as a platform for personal and authentic voice, making the marketers' behavior all the more egregious. As users of the Live Web, we are learning to a greater degree to mistrust the content we view. Even user-generated videos on YouTube are suspect. *Is it original or is it a commercial?* LonelyGirl15 seemed so real, but she was an actress playing out a script for episodic programming. No one likes being manipulated. And in this social, interactive, highly informative marketplace, the manipulators will be outed. This is the Live Web and everything is verifiable!

Interestingly, consumers don't mind being pitched by marketers if they are told up front the person giving the pitch is associated with the company or product. People will listen if they feel the agent or affiliate is providing an honest opinion, and relevant, valuable information. However, there can be a highly negative backlash from a consumer that listens openly to an agent, and then finds out after the fact that the agent hid his association with the product he was pitching.[3] Corporate authenticity is a valuable asset.

Marketing tricks serve to break consumer trust with the companies that perpetrate them. In this incredibly informative Live Webosphere, manipulations are easily dispelled. Even small marketing tricks or manipulations are foolish; they serve to harm a company by pushing consumers away rather than engaging them. So, it's not surprising that authenticity has become the keyword of this age. Authenticity isn't something that you create. It is something that you are. It starts with your company's philosophy, passion, and creed. It's developed through consistent, truthful behavior. It seeps into every person, team, and organization throughout the company. Authenticity is the core of your voice, not just for how you communicate, but what you say, do, and believe. Consumers will verify through their belief system and intuition, and through your marketing and company behavior, whether or not you are authentic.

It is authenticity that leads to credibility, credibility that enables trust, and trust which is *engaging*.

The Authentic Marketer

In this very public world we now live in, there is no room for the fake, the foolish, or the downright manipulative. If you post a commercial and try to pass it off as a user-generated video on YouTube, you will get caught. If you pay others to blog positive stories about your product, or you set up fake blogs run by your company or PR agency which are designed to look independent, you will be outed. And the tirade that follows from the general online community will hurt you much more than the possible upside the chicanery was supposed to offer. There are thousands of people on the Web who spend a great deal of their time looking for mistakes or manipulations by companies. With Digg, Reddit, Netscape, and several other user-generated news services, anyone can out a company's behavior on their blog, then link it to the news service. It then may be read by thousands of people, or picked up by mainstream news outlets.

Authentic marketing is about more than telling the truth. It is a value system, a philosophy, and set of actions. It defines your interactions with partners, customers, and the marketplace. A company, from its accounting department to the sales force, has to deliver on authenticity. You do this by being true to your company's passion and unique value proposition. Then in every way possible, offer proof points and verifiable data that supports your assertions. Today, authenticity is the key component to the marketing and communications plan.

Companies that live their passion offer a subtle but persuasive form of authenticity. Volcom management and employees have passion for the music, art, and sports that define their generation and worldview. They create a playground and products that beg like-minded people to join them. Creating a passion, and living it is the first step to becoming authentic, and enabling your audience to believe in your company and products. As companies engage audiences by becoming more porous, enabling outsiders to interact, inform, and co-create with them, authenticity becomes palpable. A sense of trust is transferred to the marketplace naturally. To be effective, open and interactive processes must be embedded in the DNA of all employees. A philosophy of engaging outsiders will allow issues to be heard, and innovative responses to be found much more quickly.

The reverse behavior is illustrated by companies with insular strategies, and employees who offer blanket rejection for anything "not invented here." Engaging companies can differentiate between proprietary information that creates competitive advantage, and insular behavior that limits a conversation with the market. Authentic companies aren't afraid to bring outsiders in, and give them a voice. If the company is doing good things, people will know and talk. If problems arise, the company has a prime opportunity to learn quickly, solve the problems, and communicate directly with its audiences. Authentic companies that openly reach outside their corporate walls, include Proctor & Gamble, Patagonia, Starbucks, Pepsico (Frito-Lay), and Coach.

Street Cred

Street cred means your company has earned trust from the marketplace, and consumers believe what you say. Once you are credible, it is easier to launch new products, and enter new markets. Gaining and maintaining credibility requires continuous focus on managing your company's life in the Webosphere, and on being consistent and transparent. Consumer voice is much louder and more convincing today than it was in 1995, in the early days of the Internet. Monitoring, interacting with, and engaging consumers where they choose to congregate are the baseline for building credibility.

Why is credibility engaging? This is a low-trust world. Too many companies do *not* deliver on their promise, and few companies surprise and delight. When others find your company credible and trust your product or brand, that creates loyalty. Customers want to buy from you again. Trusted products deliver—and the market knows it. There is an organic word-of-mouth that surrounds these products. Bloggers and customers want to comment on the product. Momentum starts. The crowd follows the old maxim, "everyone has one, I want one too." And if you think this wild behavior only happens to iPods, think again. There have been many wild successes, including Nintendo Wii, Lotus 123, Palm Pilot, and Heelys (shoes with wheels), to name a few.

Verification is what you do to ensure the marketplace views your product as credible, and credibility can set your company apart. It can make you an authority, and that makes it easier for prospects to purchase your product. *How did Apple go from being a tiny player in the PC industry (less than three-percent worldwide market share for the past six years) to the industry expert and authority on music and entertainment?* It's not just that the iPod or iPhone are great consumer electronics products. The entire company embodies the new paradigm for music: how and where to buy it, what it costs, and how to share music legally. The iPod, iPhone, and iTunes Music Store have replaced convention. Having created the new music industry, Apple has authority, and that gives the company credibility. The voice of the company leads the industry, and customers trust they will get the best product from Apple. The cycle locks in and accelerates Apple's growth.

The thing is you can't market credibility on the street. No buzz marketing campaign will make you credible. You have to earn it. Your product has to do what you say it does. Conventional wisdom now tells us that Google is where you go to search, and the iPod is the best platform for music and podcasts. The product or service becomes synonymous with the market it serves. Buzz only works if the product is credible—and it earns credibility when it delivers on its promise. So, only promise what you can deliver.

Understand that customers sense your credibility through the processes your company deploys, your customer service practices, sales practices, returns policy, and so on, as well as the behavior of your employees. Take Costco for example. The company continues to deliver the lowest prices even for products in which it could charge more. But the steadfast focus on a standard margin (a set percentage they make on each product) versus maximizing profit through margin (charging the most they can but still lower than the competition) has served customers better. Customers know they can depend on Costco to give them the best price, not just the lowest price. A similar company, Target, is increasing its customer service to better compete with Costco. In some Target stores, the company has installed a button with a promise that when pushed, an employee will appear in sixty-seconds. And an employee—smiling and ready to help—does appear in the allotted time, every time.

Once a company has street cred, few people will question the product's viability. Even better, proponents for the product—advocates— will market the product for the company.

Deliver on the Promise

Of course, verification can be in something as simple as delivering on your promises. If you create an image for your product (hip, cool, advanced, safe, quality, etc.), then it is paramount that you solidify those qualities in all of your marketing, communications, and corporate behaviors. When your customers believe the perception, they are building a trust with you. BMW, a company that produces high performance, luxury vehicles, enjoys the highly-regarded image of German quality, and the automobile offers its driver a high-success status symbol. But if small items like tail-gate light bulbs fall out, or the plastic clip that holds the sun shield up over the window breaks off, or if your dealer won't provide a rental car when the car is in for service because you didn't purchase you car from that dealership, the perception is changed. As promises are broken, or expectations are unmet, the company image crumbles.

Wells Fargo, Bank of America, and AT&T, among other credit-card companies and banks, have experienced a few chinks in their armor by the way they have handled private customer information. Since credit cards are an inherent part of everyday life in the U.S., we put our complete trust in the banks that issue them. Yet, in recent years, there have been a number of breaches of that trust. Several banks have had their customer account and personal information stolen, or they have simply lost customer data. You can't engage customers if they don't trust your company or your product.

Position your company accurately to set customer expectations. If you are a small and growing company, customers will give you more leeway with regard to customer service responsiveness or limited product features. Let customers know how you provide customer service and why. It's okay to tell people that you prefer email or chat over phone service. If the cost of phone service is too high, then choose to be exceptionally responsive via email, and make sure customers know which service is the best to use. Transparency enables customers to judge what matters most to them, and where they can accept an alternative, and it creates a valuable interaction for almost anything a company does that customers feel affects them.

There is nothing more delightful than companies that execute, and there is nothing worse than a promise unfulfilled. If you state twenty-four-hour response times, or that your product meets specific metrics, execute on the deliverables. It's always better to under promise and over deliver. Often companies get caught up with what competitors are promising, and over promise to compete. Disappointing customers is not how you want to differentiate your company. Focus on what you do well and create your own path to customers' hearts and minds.

Manage the Message

One way customers determine what your company says is true is by seeing that others are saying it. Press and bloggers give your message credibility. The influence of the mainstream press hasn't been diminished by Digg and other news aggregation sites. *The Wall Street Journal, BusinessWeek, The New York Times,* and other key business and trade publications maintain the prestige of superior research and reporting, as well as well-known staff writers and columnists. An article on your company appearing in these publications carries greater weight in the marketplace. Interestingly, coverage by these respected publications can be driven by the blogosphere. The best writers read blogs to find news and new angles. To attract the mainstream press, you will not only need advocates, early adopters, industry analysts, and possibly financial analysts backing up your story, you may also need key bloggers. These people are a new point of verification.

Inevitably there will be bad press or negative user comments. And as mentioned previously, navigating and influencing the complex Live Web environment can take a great deal of resource and time. Not only do you want to know what's being said, but you need to be prepared to manage negative comments, or a firestorm of bad news. It is so important to interact using a personal voice, and offer authentic responses— in other words, don't respond with bland, formal corporate statements. You should take every opportunity to drive viewers back to your Web site where you can provide regular updates and interactions to keep them informed.

Many PR professionals and corporate executives deeply understand how to engage editors, writers, and industry analysts. Instead of looking to place a story, they instead develop a relationship with a writer offering their time to provide background information. Writers are on deadline every day, week, or month. Anyone willing to help them fill out a story becomes a trusted partner. That often turns into attributed quotes, and then easier coverage of subjects your company is promoting. We often talk about the pitch and how to approach a writer which is still important, but it's time to talk more about how to engage the press.

Eric Schmidt while chief technology officer at Sun Microsystems was particularly adept at engaging the press. He gave writers his cellphone number and told them they could call him anytime, day or night, and he always responded quickly to their requests. Schmidt nurtured a press relationship by offering to be a background resource on their stories, and he didn't expect anything in return. Over time, he was quoted more often, and he soon became a well-known, knowledgeable source in the industry. This was valuable to Sun. But more than that, Schmidt carried these relationships through his stint at Novell and on to Google.

As CEO of Google, Schmidt has claimed that Google became a multi-billion-dollar company, creating one of the most recognized brands in the world, without marketing. He means *without advertising*. Public relations is calculated marketing, and it does cost money—and Google is a PR machine. But Schmidt's comment gives us pause. Google's entire outbound marketing budget is likely less than one percent of what it costs Coke or Pepsi to build or maintain their well-known worldwide brands through traditional advertising.[4] Google has leveraged the press and the incredible "linkedness" of the Live Web to extraordinary success.

The use, re-use, and linking of information are what inspire the Live Web. A story is useful in how it fits into a current trend, a change in thinking or behavior, or a phenomenon the marketplace wasn't previously aware of. But a story is even more useful in how it interacts with readers and links to others, and in how it invites outsiders to participate. This is one of the ways communicating has evolved driven by Live Web functionality.

Why is linking important? In academia, Ph.D. candidates write a thesis. In proposing a new idea, they *reference* previous technical papers and their authors. The most revered authors are often the most referenced. When a respected author's previous work supports a new thesis concept, the new idea is given greater credibility. If you replace the word reference with link, you have the power of the Live Web in its ability to give credibility. To become an authority and reference point, you have to offer the information, resources, and videos others want to link to. By doing this, you become the high-value resource; the place people need to go to first.

The Live Web creates a community for verification. People research what they need to know before purchasing. If you want to attract bees, you need to provide the nectar—the information they're looking for. So, it is in your company's best interest to become the information depot, and provide reliable information that is about *more* than your company and products, and that links outside your Web site to additional, reliable information. Becoming a reliable and credible source of timely information makes your company trusted, and enables customers to believe the message and positioning you use to differentiate your company.

Consumers and business purchasers know when they're being marketed to, and when they're treated as a trusted friend. They know when they're being placated, and when they've been heard. When it comes to building trust and credibility, engaging outsiders through interactive behaviors from product design, marketing, and social Web site features will do more than $100 million in advertising spending.

Influence the Influencers

There are a variety of influencers beyond the mainstream press: industry gurus, analysts, bloggers, vocal customers, affiliates, resellers, and product development partners. And customers use them as a point of verification that what you say is true. Don't expect to push your ideas out, and find willing receptors waiting. The more unique, provocative, and innovative your company is, the more work it may take to create an understanding with your target influencers. A company that offers transparency and openness, as well as easy access to useful information, gains the power of persuasion. *What are you doing to feed and care for your target influencers?*

An often untapped group of influencers are early adopters—the people that find you, try your product, and talk about it. They are often the hackers and mashers, too. The key is to attract and leverage early adopters. *Early adopters* are more curious or willing to take risk than the rest of us. They are often active users of anything new, and they like to talk about products. *Advocates* are the people who love your product and want to tell others. They can be found among early adopters or mainstream users. Since consumers are greatly influenced by other users—rather than a company's marketing—advocates are a good form of verification.

To attract early adopters, you must be offering something unique or somehow unexpected. Early adopters are fascinated by what is new and untried, and often like the prestige of using something no one else has yet. Businesses are willing to take risk with new, untried products if they believe it will give them a competitive advantage. Offering early adopters or advocates advantages like product previews, access to employees, discounts, or greater insight into product design are a great way to attract and engage them.

In the computer industry, customers will actually donate their time to make your product successful. With the advent of word-of-mouth marketing, *what is stopping a company from recruiting and managing its own group of early adopters to test and talk about its products?* Yet early adopters can provide an even more useful function. They can provide you with exactly the data you need to market your product better. You will get unabashed criticism as well as kudos, helping you discern what is most important.

How you target early adopters depends a great deal on the industry in which you work. In the computer industry, engineers are the most promising audience. They are also a great target for music, news, and cool consumer electronics, such as entertainment systems, cellphones, and cars. On average, engineers are curious, enjoy new, cool, untried gadgets, and visit lots of Web sites and blogs that talk about what's new, such as Engadget. It makes sense to go where they go to make them aware of your product. If you're in the travel industry, focus on travel enthusiasts. Not the people with the most money to book the most expensive package tour, but the person who loves searching out new places to travel to and explore, and can't wait to tell everyone when they get back. They're also more likely to share their trip photos on Flickr or Snapfish Web sites.

You need to know what early adopters are saying. Invite them into your company and Web site, and give them a place to publicly provide feedback and comments. It has gotten extremely easy to survey or poll visitors on your Web site using any number of tools: Vizu, Freepolls, Webpollscentral, or Pollmonkey. You should get as much information as you can to assess your progress, and what you may need to change. It is crucial that the company behave as transparent as possible. Early adopters are more willing to get involved with a company they can engage with and form a trust. The more responsive you are to their needs, questions, and concerns, as well as their innovative behavior around your product, the increased opportunity for them to market your product for you.

Attracting early adopters is a good start, but growing your customer base from the excited few to the mainstream marketplace takes a great deal more work. Sometimes the product is so much better than any alternative that it speaks for itself, such as Google Search or Apple's iPod. These products held such an advantage over the competition that momentum grew quickly. Most companies have to work harder to market their products and gain broad customer acceptance. This is where a consistent, strong voice matters most. It is one of the only ways to rise above the noise. Consistency also leads to credibility.

Moving from early adopter to mainstream success is one of the most trying periods a company faces, and it is often where marketing gets confused. Marketing often takes the blame when the product isn't picking up steam. *Should the story, positioning, or message change? Or, could it be that one nagging feature the product is missing?* If you have a strong story and unique differentiation, then focus at this period of time is critical. Further, staying the course and more aggressively communicating the vision and the strategy is the right path. Changes can cause confusion and weaken all of the work you've done previously, and it may even negate it. Sometimes you have to wait it out while customers get ready to buy. The Live Web can help. You can actually tune in on what early customers are saying and doing. You can communicate directly with them, and that can give you the ability to hone your plan, and stay on the offensive.

Excited customers aren't the only audience to focus on. Partners who resell your product, add value to your product, or help develop your core product are key audiences to nurture as part of your ecosystem. Although they may be given insider knowledge, often they are not encouraged to participate or interact with your marketing and communications. Partners bring a deep level of knowledge and commitment to your company, and they can help you build and extend your message to the marketplace. With a little additional effort, you can turn partners into advocates that help support your company in the real-world, and in the Web vicinities they visit. You can open up your planning wikis to partners or get their input on marketing initiatives. Pulling partners in and treating them as if they are employees creates a bond and encourages them to advocate for your company.

The image you develop, and the creed you follow must flow through everything that you do. If your message is quality, show that you source quality materials. If your message is service show *how* you go above and beyond. It's okay to outsource customer service to India, because that saves money and you can pass the savings on. But if you do, you must ensure your customer service reps are knowledgeable and have the ability to make decisions to solve the customer's problem versus being required to follow a script. External resources require the same level of training as internal resources. They have an equal ability to positively or negatively impact customers, and to become influencers. Each person in your ecosystem can impact the perception of your company.

If you want influencers in the marketplace to believe something, make sure you believe it first. Ensure that everything you are doing is consistent with the image you are developing for your product or service, as Volcom and Patagonia do.

Partners as Message-Makers

Your partners will engage with your company in an open manner if your company is authentic and trusted. Relationship building is hard work, and most companies don't spend the time enriching themselves with the true value of their partners. This value can be found in the extended human resources that offer ideas and innovations to help build your business, and in the opportunity for advocacy of your products among partner ecosystems. For this to happen, the relationship with partners needs to be open and collaborative.

If you were to analyze all of the connections your company makes with people outside its corporate walls, say, measuring the importance of the connection against the number of times communicated with daily, *what would the diagram tell you about your company? How many relationships does the company have with suppliers, partners, bloggers, consultants, designers, et al? Do you communicate most often with those people who have the most importance? Is all of the communication two-way? Is it free-form communication or controlled?* The more connected your product is, the greater number of verifications. And the more touchpoints where potential customers will see, hear, or read about your product. It is the combined effect that drives sales and momentum.

Smart companies engage affiliates, partners, and even consumers by sharing revenue and prestige. It's not just that these people become advocates and spread the word; it's a way to reach consumers through more casual, non-standard channels, in places where they will not tune out the message. Conventional business behavior teaches companies to free up resources by outsourcing to a research company, advertising agency, consulting firm, design firm, or other third party—offload work to another company and manage them. The Live Web and the collaboration tools that are fundamental to it provide the ability to pull third parties into the fold and make them part of the daily conversation. Not only will this offer better results—more creative ideas, more innovation—but it creates an ecosystem of companies that participate and communicate your story. Partners that know they are influencing or helping to create the story are more likely to help spread it.

Tools that Verify

The basics haven't changed. To back up assertions made about their products, marketers develop proof points through product demos, case studies, white papers, data sheets, and customer testimonials, then upload them to the company's Web site. These items remain flat. And in an interactive marketplace, they fail to engage. Blendtec's videos eliminate the reams of reading they could require of their audience, and instead prove their point instantly. Video has both commanding and inviting qualities. Once you've seen a Blendtec video, *what else could you possibly need to know?*

The try and buy, demo, or taste test help customers make the decision to purchase. *How can we make this process more interactive? How do we reach a larger audience or a more targeted audience?* Think ecosystem. We can no longer push our message out, and expect our audience to receive it and accept it. An ecosystem develops and takes hold through both directed and organic growth. To build an ecosystem, provide a platform that includes tools and information that others can build on such as a wiki, social site, or open APIs for the product. Through the implementation of blogs, wikis, and other interactive tools, prospects and customers can share their ideas, thoughts, experiences, and testimonials in an honest and open way. By making your demo, sample, or other materials more interesting and interactive, your audience has the opportunity to get involved. This isn't just about spreading the word, it's about starting conversations.

The social aspects of the Web make your Web site central to your ecosystem. *Is your Web site live and growing? Do prospects and customers have a place to congregate and talk to each other? Does it scream your unique value, your passion, and your creed?* Every time someone clicks on your site they should immediately know what your company stands for, and why it exists. Then they should be able to get involved. People interacting over your product provide additional proof of its adoption and momentum.

Your marketing activities pull potential customers to your Web site. Your Web site entices them to keep clicking and talking. *Now, where's the real data that will help the customer determine if they want to buy from you, or from someone else?* Be transparent. Really, consumers can find out just about anything they want to know about you somewhere else on the Internet, so why not provide all of the good, accurate data on your Web site. Transparency in and of itself is proof that you have nothing to hide, and that you deal honestly with customers. Even if your product isn't technical, provide any information someone might need or want to decide whether or not to purchase. Be specific about what is and what is not included in the purchase price. If your target audience is interested, tell them where you source your materials and where you manufacture.

Marketing today is more about participation than selling—take names, ask questions, get involved, and have fun. The new thinking is to offer free items to prospects in order to entice them into your ecosystem. At a minimum, prospects should want to give you their email address, but they have to trust you won't abuse that honor. The problem is that most companies don't follow through with the people who engage. Either the prospect liked the demo and purchased the product, or they didn't, and contact ends there. A giveaway is a customer interaction not a branding event. It is the first step in developing a relationship with the prospect. If the prospect doesn't take the next step, then provide some encouragement. Invite them to the social side of your Web site where they will have a voice, where they can get answers, and where they can get involved. Keep the conversation going so that when prospects are ready to purchase, your company is the one they think of. You can keep up the conversation by offering an RSS feeds to your blog (a constant reminder of your company that shows up on their desktop daily), through additional free information or reports, or through fun activities that are engaging such as contests or games.

Measurability

As discussed in Chapter Three, measurability is one of the key attributes of a persuasive customer value proposition. You can measure most product attributes, such as performance, quality, strength, and durability. If you can't measure an attribute, think twice about promoting it. Of course, style can't be measured, and it certainly can be a differentiator. So, you have to use good judgment. If the value you are marketing can be measured and proven, then you have an influential tool for selling your product. If it's difficult to measure up against your competition, then narrow your metrics to a specific niche or type of customer in order to optimize results, and show metrics in which you lead.

Measurement often requires significant resources. If you're going to directly compare your product to the competition with results that can be measured—rather than using conjecture and hyperbole—then you have to purchase and use the competitors' products. The up front investment in a program that measures real-life results is more than worthwhile, because measurability is a potent tool for verification and customer adoption. The good thing is that in most industries, analysts perform benchmark studies and analyses that can verify your assertions. Often, customers are willing to make available their internal benchmark results. Both of these options save you time and money.

What if your product is highly complex or expensive? How can you get your customers involved? If you can't demo the product, you want to find a way for customers to feel as if they have experienced the product in some way. Often we use customer testimonials to show prospects how the product is used in real life, and the value customers have experienced. But when the expense is high, prospects want to know how the product will work in their environment. The next best thing is a simulation—a small software tool that allows a customer to plug in their business variables, and determine if your product solves their problem.

A tool of this type can provide competitive comparisons, or illustrate how the customer will save money, work faster, or create new business opportunities. A software tool can provide an interactive or even immersive connection with a prospect. Companies spend millions developing a product, but often are unwilling to spend a few more dollars to develop the tools needed to engage customers, and get them to purchase. A software tool enables the customer to validate your marketing message, and find a deeper level of verification on your product. Taking this extra step can persuade your customers to choose to buy your product quickly, or even pay a higher price.

Getting from Truth to Proof

It's difficult to believe that the causes of and results from the greenhouse effect were described by Swedish chemist, Svante Arrhenius, in *1896*. The reality of global warming took *one-hundred-and-ten* years to reach a tipping point. This long process reminds us that facts often aren't enough to sway opinion. From the 1930s to the 1970s, the techniques and calculations used to prove the *greenhouse effect*—where carbon dioxide emissions increase global warming—greatly improved. This enabled scientific proof of the year-over-year rise in greenhouse gases, and its negative effect on the environment. Yet, nothing happened. Reputable scientists couldn't get the press to cover this dramatic story. This was partly due to the fact that some scientists argued the atmosphere was cooling. *Was it getting hotter or colder?* The confused message drowned out both messages.

Finally, in 1990, there was consensus. Forty-nine Nobel-prize-winning scientists and seven-hundred National Academy of Sciences members signed an appeal stating that the Earth's natural greenhouse effect was amplified by the buildup of various gases introduced by human activity, and that it has the potential to create dramatic changes in climate. Hundreds of scientists from around the world agreed on the estimates of the range of global warming. You would think that would have done it, that all mainstream news outlets would cover the story, and companies and people around the world would have started to curb their destructive behavior.

We would have to wait another sixteen years. The biggest impact on the lack of adoption of (or belief in) the global warming trend was due to the brilliant marketing tactics of the naysayers, *and* the lack of persuasive marketing tactics coming from the scientific community. Amazingly, over one-thousand scientists from around the world could not gain credibility because well-known politicians, and radio and TV show hosts used their bully pulpits to raise doubt, create confusion, and successfully ridicule the experts. Confusion has the power to make even the most obvious truth, questionable. When Al Gore, the forty-fifth United States Vice President, took on the cause, the tide started to change. (It's a bit more difficult to call Al Gore a "hippie dippie wacko," the term applied to the scientists.) Gore and his team reaped the benefits of the socially-networked Live Web (which gave greater visibility and credibility to the science and research), created an ecosystem of educated communicators, and produced a video—which became a movie—and a tipping point was reached.[5]

Vanity Fair began running its annual Green issue, CNN started its Planet in Peril segments, and countless companies including Wal-Mart, General Electric, and Sony, among others began touting their green programs. Yvon Chouinard's One Percent for the Planet, a fund any company can donate to, was mentioned more often in the press, and Chouinard found himself on the cover of *Fortune* magazine's Green issue. Today, there are dozens of Web sites and blogs providing tips to consumers and businesses for saving the environment, e.g., Ideal Bite, Treehugger, WorldChanging, Gristmill, and Inhabitat, to name a few. Anyone can determine their personal carbon footprint—their carbon dioxide output that hurts the environment—so that they can lower it or pay for it. There is an entire generation of students graduating from college determined to work only for companies that care for the planet, or build their own companies where they can create something of value and help the environment at the same time.

Often truth doesn't win, *persuasion* does. The scientists couldn't find a platform to persuade the masses that global warming is here even when 1998 and 2002 were the hottest years on record. Proof is the starting point to persuade the marketplace. An open, authentic platform that invites others to get involved helps to establish an idea. The highly-focused, highly-visible message, such as an Oscar-award-winning movie, certainly helps.

To be persuasive, start by being verifiable and credible. If you can provide verification that what you say is true, you will gain attention from your customers. If customers can verify for themselves that what you say is true, you will gain great loyalty. Verifying your unique value proposition removes a huge roadblock for prospects since they have little trust in marketers, and are forced to spend their time reading, researching, and talking with you and others trying to determine if what you're marketing is truthful.

How do customers know if what you say is true? There are a number of ways they can choose to inform themselves via the Web, either by asking customer experts, reading general customer comments, or reading trusted sources such as press or blogger posts. Consumers naturally feel there is wisdom in crowds so market momentum is one of the best forms of credibility, but that assumes your product has jumped the chasm from early adopter to mainstream customers. Becoming credible takes time and perseverance, and a real commitment to your vision. If you deliver on your promises, you will find the journey much easier to travel.

Authenticity is a business model. The image you build must continually be proven out by all that you do and all that you are. Credibility is built over time through continuous good actions. You can't just sprinkle some on like pixie dust and hope it will fly. If you can create the information and tools prospects need to verify, then you will make believers out of them. When you are consistent, the image sticks.

6

KNOW YOUR VICINITY

MANAGING THE ONLINE LIFE OF YOUR BRAND IS
LIKE BREATHING OXYGEN; YOU DO IT
CONTINUOUSLY OR YOU WON'T SURVIVE.

Historically brands were built through TV and print ads. Today, Web 2.0 is the bedrock in which products, image, and differentiation are created. Without a strategy that incorporates the Live Web as fundamental to branding, and requires monitoring and managing your brand's manifestation across the Web, companies will find it impossible to influence the purchase decision or persuade audiences to participate in their ecosystem. The rules for marketing products and communicating with target audiences have changed. Anyone can research your company and products, and more than reading negative customer comments, they can find out if you're doing harm to the environment, using child labor in a foreign country, or providing poor customer service. The Web is a place where brand perceptions and reality collide, and companies need to be prepared for the fallout.

In this age, managing your brand means understanding your audience's worldview, one that is greatly defined by the online neighborhoods and meeting places they choose to visit. These Live Web vicinities, whether they are blogs, social networking sites, product comparison sites, or user opinion sites change audience behavior, learning, and perceptions. This new online world is where individuals find community, belonging, conversation, and self-expression. Harnessing these core elements of audience behavior will give companies the skills to manage their brands successfully. Marketers must know where people choose to interact and congregate, and what they do and say in order to impact their customers' experience. In addition, companies can take much better advantage of the ecosystems and vicinities built by their partners, resellers, and affiliates in order to broaden their audience interactions.

Vicinity encompasses the neighborhoods and communities where people meet on the Web, what they do there, and what impacts their choices. These vicinities are also media vehicles for placing ads or other marketing programs which is covered in detail in the next chapter. Managing vicinity—monitoring and interacting—helps us understand brand perception and loyalty as it is linked to conversation, community, advocacy, and influence. Over managing or trying to control these online norms and behaviors can lead to disaster as FedEx learned through the box furniture fiasco (Chapter Seven), and Coca-Cola learned through the Mentos/Diet Coke folly.

The social aspects of the Live Web encourage people to organize along shared interests, such as pets, health, diet and nutrition, video games, or technology. Brand is secondary. Customers set the rules; they don't want someone pushing or driving the conversation, as marketers often try to do. They want information without a catch, and they expect companies to share information and ideas. Today it is just as important to be a trusted information resource as it is to have brand leadership. It is also imperative that marketers adjust their scope from targeting the mass market or segmented market to the individual. We have the ability to learn more about users than ever before possible, either by tracking their clicks or by interacting and engaging them through online communities. And although online audience metrics aren't as straight forward to track as zip codes and home values, the possibility to know so much more about users, their behavior, and what influences them is at our fingertips.

Whether you sell direct or through third parties, there has never been a better time to interact with and gather information about your prospects and customers directly. We can only approximate what a consumer does in front of their television, but we *know* what a specific individual does on their computer. We can track their clicks from the step before they enter our Web site to the step after they leave, then group individuals who have similar online behaviors at any given time. By knowing what site they came from or which search term they used (from which search engine), we can determine where our audience learns, how serious they are about purchasing, and what type of promotion would work best for them.

When it comes to homing in on customers, we have moved from demographics, psychographics, and long-drawn-out behavioral research studies to online behavioral targeting. The thing about demographics is that zip code and home values tell us something about a purchaser's *likely* behavior. Companies target arts and antiques to million-dollar home owners, and they target high-interest loans to residents of low-income housing or apartments, because they *assume* wealthy individuals have enough discretionary income to purchase art, and low-income individuals need a loan badly enough to pay exorbitant rates. Online behavior, however, separates what a person may do with what a person actually is doing. The more we learn about where they go online, whether that is social networking sites, Web TV sites, online games, or technical blogs, the easier it is to find and target them with the best offer at the right moment.

As we learn to continuously monitor and manage our brands online and interact with individual behaviors, there are a few new rules marketers should employ. First, you don't want to respond directly to negative comments on your products or company. Let the community converse openly. To influence the conversation, marketers should develop a large and active group of advocates who can respond naturally on their behalf. Second, you must respond quickly to real product issues, flaws, or disasters when they are raised by bloggers, mainstream press, or customers (or anyone, for that matter). There are many choices for how to respond. The CEO can write a post on her blog, or an employee closest to the issue can respond in a personable tone explaining how the company will resolve the issue. Executives must refrain from sending out formal, lawyer-approved statements. They go against the norms and natural informality of social networks and blogs. Marketers can use these events as a chance to reveal the human side of their company, and exemplify the company's values and commitment to great products and service. Third, marketers should develop a deeper relationship with corporate lawyers to understand what truly impacts trademark ownership. If someone uses your product boxes to make furniture and puts pictures on the Web or talks about it on social sites, does that really degrade the rights you have over your trademark? Going forward, flexibility with your brand will be critical. When users are engaged so much that they play with your brand (versus your competitors) find a way to use their efforts as part of your marketing.

"Markets are conversations" is the provocative statement made by Doc Searls and David Weinberger in their book *The Cluetrain Manifesto* years before the Live Web showed us how true this is. These conversations now take place online. It's the conversation that can change your business, and it is imperative that you get involved. Any Web site, blog, or wiki where people interact and communicate has the potential to help or hurt the sales of your product. Understanding how, when, and where users self-organize, create, search, converse, and comment helps marketers determine how to reach them, participate in their conversations, and ultimately create influence. As we have discussed, the cultural phenomenon of public user-expression, user-generated content, and consumer authority, significantly impacts the methods marketers should deploy to join and influence the conversation.

The Era of the Individual

Google's PageRank democratized the Web; Digg democratized news; and YouTube democratized entertainment. And yes, we are facing the democratization of marketing. Users create and upload videos for entertainment. They open up proprietary platforms to add functions, or they mash together two applications. Today, consumers have an unprecedented level of influence in their relationship with marketers. They can choose to opt in to receive your message or black-box your email (send it to the spam folder, delete, or ignore it). And as we're all aware, they have the capacity to complain about products or companies in wide-reaching public forums. It is critical at this juncture that marketing organizations accept the cultural change and the transfer of power. This is the era of the individual and even the wealthiest and most successful marketers must negotiate unusual waters.

Whether you call them consumers, prosumers, hobbyists, hackers, or mashers, individuals are becoming more a part of the product process. Just because we as marketers say the product is done, doesn't mean customers feel the need to take us at our word. People hack, manipulate, add to, combine, and otherwise "enhance" our products to fit their specific needs, or just for fun and entertainment. Hackers can add value to your product that you haven't thought of yet. *Hacking* (once a dirty word) involves opening up, changing, or adding to your product to personalize or customize it. Hackers find products they like, and evolve them to meet their needs. Good thing, because other people have similar needs, and can take advantage of the hack. Hackers are engaged. They add to your product's social ecosystem. Those of us that download hacks or mashups are participating in the user-generated community.

Apple's iPod is a closed system, yet hundreds of hackers have opened up the iPod and written unauthorized applications to run on the music player. These hobbyists can easily pool their ideas and share their applications in online communities. The outsider behavior places one of the world's best marketers in a sticky situation—either support or deny the enthusiasts. Certainly, there is no more confusion over the impact of the Live Web, and the people who use it, on marketing. Hobbyists also extend the prosumer (professional consumer) concept by making customers a part of the ecosystem that creates value around your product. Instead of trying to eliminate or control hacker behavior (unless, of course, the hacks are meant to reveal intellectual property or hurt the market), you can get involved, open your product's interfaces, and create a collaborative platform. Open and collaborative companies draw committed and loyal audiences.

Content, tools, technology, and entertainment are developed by individuals for the purpose of self-expression, reputation, recognition, appreciation, attention, amusement, and simply to fill extra hours in the day. This hobbyist culture is an example of how contagious the Live Web can be. Kids growing up today no longer bother with CDs, film, or camcorder tape, and adults are moving in the same direction. Digital information can be moved, mashed, and shared in an instant. The idea of having all of your data out there on the Webosphere is comforting. (Okay, it's scary, too.) You can get to it wherever you are. You can share it, link it, tag it, and allow others to add value to it. The connectedness is infectious. No wonder millions of people are taking advantage of their new-found community.

User empowerment and expression is great context for how we frame the conversation with audiences going forward. There isn't much marketers can take for granted anymore, including the look of their Web site. There are applications that give users (even non-techies) exceptional control over changing the look and feel of a company's Web site. Greasemonkey makes it possible for users to change how a specific Web-site page displays—most likely in a way the company had not intended. One prominent example is Amazon pages which can be made to display price comparisons. Greasemonkey can be used to permanently remove ads, change layout design, or display feeds in a floating panel.[1] Further, consumers can design their own home page on Google or Yahoo, and by incorporating your company's RSS feed and other feeds about your company or industry, learn all about you without ever visiting your Web site or experiencing your brand. Independence from accepting what marketers offer, the way they offer it, has become a theme of the Live Web.

This sense of independence consumers feel has generated a culture that takes advantage of the grand soap box that is the Live Web. You, me, and anyone else can create or join an online community, and use it to air complaints or promote products. Brand advocates, bloggers, and consumers all have something in common: the desire to express their views. And they now have a platform to be heard by thousands, tens of thousands, or millions of people. Additionally, people with unrecognized talent now have a forum to promote themselves, as did the budding videographers who produced Lonelygirl15 and uploaded episode after episode to YouTube, or the performing artists who drew millions of viewers to their video illustrating what happens when you drop Mentos (the candy) into Diet Coke. (It explodes.) They posted the video on their EepyBird Web site, and it was quickly posted on Revver and YouTube where it went viral. A quick search on Google employing the terms "Coke Mentos" returns almost 1.5 million results. A search for the same terms on YouTube turns up over eight-thousand videos. These weren't ad guys looking for new accounts, or to make a name for themselves; they were just creating entertainment.

The user-generated Coke-Mentos video received news coverage in the *Wall Street Journal* and *BusinessWeek*, was on the cover of *Ad-Age*, and the creators appeared on the *Late Show with The David Letterman*. The viral video even found a permanent place in history on Wikipedia. The Coca-Cola Company's response was initially indignant. They clearly didn't like someone out of their control playing with their brand. They demanded YouTube take down the video. As you might expect, the negative backlash from the online community was huge, and Coke's management was publicly flogged by the mainstream press.[2] Coke's experience taught the company and the rest of us that brand flexibility is required on the Live Web.

It's not simply the lunatic fringe and college students driving change. Working adults (even people over forty!) go home at night and have a blast mashing songs, tinkering with their Lego Mindstorms (robots), and making videos to post on YouTube.[3] The Baby-Boomer generation is no longer sitting in the back seat. They are vocal about products they advocate and those they think should be killed. They extensively research products online before they purchase, and they are avid users of social networking, blogs, and price comparison sites. Adults are learning the advantages of the social Webosphere from the young and adventurous, namely that online strangers are friends, and friends are what make you connected, popular, and interesting. The early adopters have also taught the rest of us that *anyone* can become popular or empowered with a little ingenuity and dedication. Think about it, Toronto-based, twelve-year-old Adam Fuhrer, by obsessively reading and linking news he finds on the Web, has built such a following that he has become one of the most influential individuals in determining what news is important enough to make the front page of Condé Nast's Reddit news site (which is similar to Digg).[4]

Before the Live Web was taking form, there were signs of cultural change. Reality TV shows Survivor, The Biggest Loser, American Idol, and America's Funniest Videos were outperforming prime-time sitcoms and dramas. People are interested in what other, *real* people are saying and doing. And if we accept this change and incorporate it into our marketing, we can listen, learn, and adapt. We can find our target audience in the places they visit, monitor their behavior, and learn to influence and engage them. Additionally, we can allow them to express themselves, show their individualism, and join groups we've created for them, all in an effort to strengthen our brand.

Beyond Demographics

Rachel (our fictitious person) is in the market to buy a car. She searches on the terms "2007 cars," "sedans," and "fuel efficient cars." Her results get her clicking on several branded automobile Web sites. She then takes a look at *Consumer Reports* online to see how the cars stack up for safety, quality, and value. Later, she is clicking through the Sierra Club site and evaluating her carbon dioxide footprint on SafeClimate.

net. All of these clicks tell us a lot about Rachel right now. And to dig a little deeper we can also analyze the path she takes from one set of information to another, how long she visits a page of content relative to the amount of content on the page, if she clicks on specific products or data, and the behaviors of like-minded people. Putting all of these behaviors together, we can determine she is in the market to buy a new, cost-effective, safe car that is a hybrid or highly fuel efficient. This type of behavioral targeting takes us light years beyond demographics, a method for determining what someone *may* purchase based on their zip code, home value, and income.

There's also more to it than just online clicks. We can determine if an individual is a hobbyist (likes to create and upload products or information online for reputation), minipreneur (makes money as an affiliate, or joins pay-for-creation sites), content-generator (enjoys creating entertainment and personal pages for social sites), or passive viewer (likes to see what everyone else is doing). These additional behaviors can determine a marketers approach in an ad or offer. It is simply easier and more effective to join a conversation when you know more about the people who are already talking. Behavioral targeting and social networking interactions teach marketers what kinds of programs and interactions make sense for prospects and customers. The Live Web gives us an exceptional opportunity to connect and engage at this deeper level.

Search, Social, and Web TV

Online vicinities are places people visit most often to interact with others. Search, although not social (yet), has become the standard launching point for billions of conversations. Search is a platform for advertising, but with billions of queries every day, it is where most people begin a dialogue—where they start their discovery process on the way to purchasing a product—which makes search the prevailing lead generation mechanism. This is one paradigm that can't be ignored. Optimizing your Web site, product pages, blog, or any online communications for search is critical. And although Google is still the king of search, the marketplace is changing. There are well over one-hundred search engines and search sites designed or optimized for different purposes. *Meta-search* engines collate the results from other search engines. A meta-search engine does not maintain its own database of Web pages. Instead, a search request typed into a meta-search box is sent to other search engines where results are pulled from their Web databases. Some meta-search companies include, Dogpile, Zuula, PlanetSearch, and GoshMe. There are video (Blinkx, PureVideo), audio (FindSounds), and image (Pixsy) search engines. And there are social (Collarity, Filangy, Omgili, Sproose), podcast (Podzinger, Blabline), mobile (Netvibes2Go, Yahoo! Onesearch, Ask Mobile, Slifter), RSS feed (WASALive!), and blog-specific (Blogdigger, Gigablast, IceRocket, Sphere) search engines. Some search engines are designed just to find people. And some are optimized for charity, shopping, and specific countries.

Each one of these environments presents an opportunity where your audience can find you. The higher up your company appears in results pages, the more value users apply to it. *The company must be doing something right.* Search engine optimization (SEO) has spawned an industry of tradeshows, bloggers, books, and vendors—and for good reason. Entire businesses have been built on the back of top-of-page search results. With the mass movement toward using search to find any product or service, where your product shows up in the results list can mean life or death. Getting top-of-page results takes hard work and time, but don't stop at your home page or with Google. Optimize all of your company's Web pages, blogs, and feeds, and determine the mix of search engines that will bring users to you. If you're only optimizing for search engines that visitors come from today, then you may be missing out on search engine sites where your company doesn't yet appear in results, and the people who use those sites won't find you.

Often when users search they aren't going to land on your Web page but on a comparison, comment, or blog site where they can find out more about a product or service first. These vicinities are helping to shift purchasing power to the consumer. Just take a quick look at Yelp, BazaarVoice, RateItAll, Become, PlanetFeedback, or Review Centre, where you can see that consumers believe other consumers over marketers. Each of these sites illustrate that when significant numbers of people comment on any specific product or subject, the abundance of comments influence the conversation, giving it greater impact on the marketplace. Rarely do you have one person with enough influence that they alone can change buying patterns—except Oprah, of course. Often it is the volume of comments that creates change.

Whatever your product category, find the blogs and community-rating sites that follow it, and monitor them in real-time. But more than that, get involved in the conversation and be a useful agent of information. So when an issue arises, you can respond quickly and in the tone and language of the community. But remember, people are allowed to have opinions. You shouldn't respond to every negative comment. These communities are great places to learn about your products, service, and sales, and how they are being received. You can also determine if people understand your voice, story, and creed. It can tell you a great deal about who *they* see as your biggest competition.

Social networking sites, blogs, podcasts, Wikipedia, file sharing sites, virtual worlds, user-review sites, and consumer-comment sites are just the beginning of the consumer-generated online world. Consumer-generated content has catalyzed businesses and communities across the Web. Social networking sites are now vast in number. Beyond MySpace, Facebook, and Xanga, there are dozens of sites designed for specific audiences such as dog lovers (Dogster), auto enthusiasts (CarDomain), and church leaders (MyChurch). Determining whether or not you should advertise on these sites depends on your product, target audience, and strategy. Social sites aren't just for teenagers anymore. The average age on MySpace is now thirty-five years old with a growing audience over forty.[5] Social sites will eventually replace user groups as a place purchasers (consumers or business) will gather to connect, create, and converse. Social is a way of thinking and behaving, not just a destination.

Online games create interactive, online vicinities that can no longer be ignored by marketers. Game players are almost forty percent women, and the average age is also increasing reaching thirty-three in 2007.[6] Some companies use online games as a form of communication between employees. As mentioned before, Best Buy's Geek Squad's technical support reps toss around ideas, or discuss customer problems while playing an online game. Although counter-intuitive, playing games at work can actually increase productivity. In some online games, marketers can advertise by pasting their brand up like wallpaper somewhere in the game—but that would be missing the point. Games are storylines. The best way to reach gamers is to align with the game and become part of the content. Marketers need to find a way to extend the user's experience, and play the game by their rules. This is the Marketing 2.0 approach. It's not just about the ad. It's about the experience you create that compliments the environment you are entering.

And that brings us to Web TV. Several different strategies have been deployed for this new platform. YouTube is filled with user-generated content, and designed to be highly social. Users post video of their kitten sleeping, their own Tae Kwon Do expertise, or a provocative presentation on world change. Joost, Yahoo!'s The 9, and Veoh are designed as online networks for professionally-developed content. They create and air short-form, episodic programming or entertainment programming (think Entertainment Tonight). Heavy, SuperDeluxe, and blip.tv offer a mix of professionally-developed content and user-generated content. These sites focus on entertainment and social networking.

No matter the format, the biggest mistake Web TV companies and marketers can make is to maintain conventional advertising on this new platform. Pre-roll and post-roll advertising (spots that run right before or after the video) don't work well. Thirty-second and sixty-second spots slotted around content are too long for Internet audiences. Push messaging takes creativity and ingenuity to get noticed. Marketing needs to be brief, informative, and entertaining, or connect the viewer to something they want to interact with. The idea isn't "tell them everything" because they are a captive audience—because they no longer are. The change in format is to entice, surprise, or delight, *and then* get them to extend their current experience. And if you think this is a lot more work, welcome to Marketing 2.0 and the Live Web. You can target customers right where they play and interact on the Web, but you can no longer successfully push out a mass message. The message needs to be tuned into the individual and the vicinity.

Building Community

Today, it is simple for a company to make available basic tools and user policies, and enable people to build a community on a subject that interests or informs. MySpace, YouTube, and Digg are nothing more than platforms where users create all of the information, communication, and entertainment. Smart companies are finding ways to leverage these tools and build communities. CNET Networks, Inc. has developed several community sites that are interactive and based on the collective wisdom of viewers. A few of their sites include Chowhound, Webshots, and GameSpot. CNET has essentially rewritten the rules for online magazines. While too many businesses and publishing companies repurpose their printed content for online use, CNET has taken a new approach, creating original content that fits the viewer, and making it painless for viewers to enhance or create their own content.

Hitachi Data Systems (HDS) set up the Data Storage Industry Wiki. This site offers no branding or self-serving behavior by HDS. Instead anyone in the industry can learn from or educate others. Categories on the wiki include everything from blogs and podcasts to research, price lists, and job postings. *Why host a site you don't control?* When companies step up to this role, they become a trusted partner, and position the company as a leader. They are the company building the foundation that other companies or people add value to. In this way, companies can help create the conversation, and then participate in the community as a trusted information authority. Marketers have the opportunity to create community where none exists and bring people together. If you make a community self-serving, that will diminish the intended results. You want to build image, reputation, and relationships first. People will see your subject knowledge, passion, and commitment, and this is what builds credibility, trust, and influence.

Influence over Control

Managing in an environment where consumers have so much power is certainly complex. Your job is to allow your brand and your products participate, and to give up some control in order to capture the public's unabashed enthusiasm. However, you don't want to give up complete control over your brand. You certainly don't want your products to appear on XXX-rated sites (unless of course that's what you intended). You don't want a pissed-off customer to coral their friends and make your product look bad on Amazon or Shopper.com. There is a way to manage the social Web without sending out thousands of cease-and-desist letters.

Develop a strategy for how you will communicate and how you will respond to an individual's undesired behavior. Most of it can and should be ignored. Companies that raise a fuss over an article from one lone blogger in Omaha draw much greater visibility to the subject in the first place. In the Live Web, people get to say what they think. Your job is to develop the broadest group of advocates possible so that they can respond on your behalf. Their sheer enthusiasm will displace negative comments. There are times when it will be important that you respond. When you do, replace the faceless, corporate persona with a voice that fits the vicinity you're communicating within. If you are already participating and communicating in many social environments across the Web, this is much easier to do.

The best form of influence is a repeated message by a variety of people coming from a number of places. You can get this result by using online communities to get your message, vision, and story heard and understood, and by inviting enthusiastic users to participate. They don't have to produce your ads. And you don't have to encourage their wacky behavior with contests unless that's a good fit for your marketing. You do have to be whole-heartedly enthusiastic about what they are doing, and to do that you must be a great deal more open. Smart companies apply resources to monitoring social-networking sites, price-comparison sites, and any other outlets where users are providing their comments. Their influence is buoyed by the knowledge and insights they gain from these interactions. The best path is to learn from activities on the Live Web and leverage user behavior without trying to control it.

Partners, Advocates, and Affiliates

Here's the rub. Apple and Google are anomalies. If your strategy is to create a breakthrough of that magnitude, that's no different than a personal retirement strategy that depends on winning the lottery. Most companies need to build an ecosystem of partners and friends to gain momentum. The problem is that we've become complacent, and continue to treat partners in an old-fashioned manner. A *partner* is anyone outside your company that helps you create, market, or sell your product. Those are core functions to a business's very existence, yet often these activities are outsourced, meaning they are chopped up and given to the company with the best bid. Then, that company is managed as a separate, distant entity. The impact can be slower time-to-market, increased cost, and minimized innovation. As previously discussed, Live Web technologies can be cost-effectively used to openly collaborate with partners, truly bring them into the fold. In this way, they can become a competitive advantage helping to innovate and add value or differentiation to your products.

Resellers—the sales arm of a company—are often treated as outsiders and simple box pushers. They are trained by a company to sell and support their products. Then the resellers are handed completed marketing materials, and told to go meet with customers. Resellers are referred to as a *channel* of distribution, and often we treat them as nothing more. In a company without a direct sales force, resellers are the lifeblood, the people interfacing with your customers. *Doesn't it make sense to make them a core part of the company?* It also makes sense to take better advantage of their value-add. To differentiate their business, resellers are learning to create communities, express their own views, and determine their own language for speaking with their audience. They carry their own brand name and often sell multiple brand products. They choose to create a platform of their own—a way to differentiate themselves and add value. Since resellers are on the front lines interacting with your customer, they are an essential community to be influenced and valued. The ecosystem they build is one in which you want to become a principal player.

Resellers are a custom community that your company hand-picked. It only makes sense that they become a core member of your business. The way to do this is to treat partners as advocates, as people who will build or extend your product or service. A great way to nurture resellers (or any partner) is to develop a real-time feedback system via a wiki—a place where they can provide ideas and offer feedback on products and programs coming from your company. This will enable you to pull partners inside the company, and make them a part of the team. Further, you can make sure they are "in the know" as much as possible by getting them early trials of new products and early access to company news and marketing campaigns so they can extend the buzz.

Affiliates can also be an extension of the company, its marketing efforts, and revenue generation. For a share of the revenue or flat fee payments, affiliates promote your product, often on their Web sites or blogs, providing broader visibility and potential sales. Sharing revenue with affiliates is fast becoming a key business model of the Live Web. Widgets are helping the affiliate model to expand quickly. GoodStorm, FavoriteThingz, and MyPickList all offer a widget that enables anyone to sell their favorite music or products from their personal Web site, MySpace, or Facebook page, and take a cut of the revenue.[7] And, of course, Amazon offers revenue sharing through their associates program where Web-site owners and publishers can post Amazon products on their Web site or blog and earn extra dollars from sales. By making a widget available for download, or providing a simple sign-up process, companies can experience organic growth of their affiliate base. They can extend their brand, cost-effectively increase their sales, and influence a group of customers that have become advocates.

Another new business model includes paying for content or sharing ad revenue with content creators. Many sites pay customers a flat fee to enhance the information on their site, including Scoopt and SpyMedia which pay for photographs, and Daytipper which pays for useful tips on subjects ranging from relationships and cooking to technology. Revver, Break.com, MetaCafe, and Flixya share as much as fifty-percent of ad revenue with anyone who creates content for their sites. YouTube also shares revenue, but limits it to the top tier user-generated video producers.[8] Revenue-sharing is a business model that draws a large audience of *minipreneurs*[9] to participate in the brand and build the value and differentiation.

Whether it is resellers, affiliates, or advocates, companies that create community around the people who love their products or service enough to promote it to other people or even help sell the product will empower their ecosystem.[10] Creating advocates means providing the forums—Web site pages, wikis, and blogs—for them to communicate regularly with you and each other, and responding to their needs and input. It means sharing information and recognition, and respecting their space and personal identity, while at the same time, not forcing your ideas or message upon them. Advocates want to express themselves and their opinions in their own words with their own creativity, and for this to happen, marketers have to be open and flexible.

Each company based on its products, industry, and market position will become part of a specific set of vicinities on the Web. Get involved, monitor, and manage the conversations to start, then interact with advocates, prosumers, minipreneurs, and affiliates to take your company to the next level. Embrace flexibility with your brand so that outsiders can play and add to its evolution.

7

DRIVE THE VEHICLE (DON'T LET THE VEHICLE DRIVE YOU)

THE DEBATE BETWEEN TRADITIONAL AND DIGITAL
MARKETING IS OVER. IF THE PROJECT DOESN'T
HAVE A DIGITAL ELEMENT, KILL IT.

Marketing 2.0 fundamentally reinvents marketing as a *distributed experience*. Pieces of your message reach your audience via dozens of vehicles both online and off. Some of the vehicles in which your brand and message appear are under your control, but not all of them. There is a new level of complexity that needs to be mastered. You push your message, consumers pull it, adapt it, re-communicate it, and somehow, you need to connect all these dots, and paint a cohesive picture.

TV commercials, print ads, direct mail, catalogs, billboards, and other traditional marketing formats aren't going away (at least anytime soon). That means you must choose the optimal vehicle to meet the objectives in your strategy, and ensure that your message connects many times with audiences through different forums. Digital (online) marketing may take the lead or it may support your offline initiatives. It adds an interactive dimension otherwise not possible.

There is a vast array of on online marketing vehicles to choose from including your Web site, email campaigns, paid search, banner ads, search engine optimization, widgets, video, and word-of-mouth campaigns. Online includes marketing to cellphone users and inside virtual worlds, as well as how you incorporate Live Web technologies including tagging, voting, RSS, wikis, blogs, podcasts, and more. Each audience touchpoint, whether online or off, is designed to relate or connect to produce a snowball effect. And no matter where or how your message or content appears, the goal is to drive viewers to interact with your brand, or take the next step.

The next step can encompass a range of activities, but we can now assume most everyone you target will have access to a computer and a cellphone, and that the next step will likely involve one of those two items. The purpose of the digital element in marketing programs is to capture individuals as long-term participants. You want to give them the opportunity to interact with the product or company, download additional information on their cellphone or computer, or participate in a contest or event. The advantages that digital gives us is the ability to gather names and email addresses for future contact, and to track audience behavior as they interact with your offline and online activities.

We're starting to see the integration of traditional and digital in big places. CNN's Anderson Cooper reminds viewers after each segment to get more information on CNN.com or to give him feedback on his Anderson Cooper 360° blog. *Vanity Fair* points readers to the VF.com Web site to get more information on the subject of the story they've just read. Driving offline viewers online allows a company to engage its audience with more information and interactivity, capturing their minds and potentially their wallets. The digital element of offline marketing programs is designed to get a prospect or customer back on the Web and back to your site.

Online marketing programs such as ads or paid search are also designed to get viewers back to your Web site. The page you send users to from an ad—the *landing page*—should always be a cohesive next step in their process of learning and engaging. The page must be informative, interesting, and open to user interactivity such as comments and tags. For the online vicinities your prospects or customers visit that you don't control, there are opportunities to bring viewers back to you. The key is to develop advocates or evangelists that help maintain eyes and ears on the Web, commenting and pointing viewers to the correct information or Web site. And, as stated in the previous chapter, that means you need to find and nurture early adopters and customers as brand advocates, as well as develop blogger and possibly affiliate networks to help extend and enhance your communications.

Use the Web, Not Lawyers

As mentioned early in this book, brand control is an illusion. How you respond to the disaggregation of *your* brand from *your* content affects how *your* company is viewed in the marketplace. We are at the beginning of how users will interact with our brands and marketing. Companies that are flexible, open, and interactive, and incorporate Marketing 2.0 early, will find it much easier to adapt in this new world. *What will you do when your trademarks and copyrighted materials show up somewhere on the Web without your approval and out of context?* First and foremost, don't allow your lawyers to lead the response, as FedEx did in the following example.

Jose Avila was scraping together nickels and dimes to get by. After moving to Arizona for a new job, he didn't have the money to buy furniture for his apartment. With the ingenuity and creativity of a young interior designer, he built his desk, bed, couch, table, and chairs using FedEx boxes, then he posted pictures on his website, fedexfurniture. com. In just twenty-four hours, FedEx lawyers sent Jose threatening letters requiring he pull down the Web site due to copyright and trademark infringement.[1] The highly useable box furniture was a clear testament to the strength of FedEx boxes, and offered a strong message that customers would enjoy peace of mind shipping their goods in them. You would think FedEx could find positive leverage here (or just ignore the whole thing). But the lawyers took charge, and the market's response to FedEx's behavior was punishing. Stories about FedEx's take-down notice for Avila's Web site hit the mainstream press, and the makeshift box furniture received a great deal more exposure than otherwise likely. FedEx had backed itself into a corner, underestimated the influence of the Live Web, and completely missed a valuable opportunity for building on their core message.

Without resorting to legal warfare or simply throwing up your hands in disgust, use the chaos of the Live Web to drive positive outcomes. If FedEx had been Marketing 2.0-savvy, the company would have captured Avila and his friends using the furniture in a provocative and fun video, and uploaded it to YouTube with the message, *boxes so tough, you can live on them.* In other words, your valuable items won't get destroyed when shipped to their destination via FedEx. Define a clear plan for how you will respond to users that go beyond your comfort zone. It's not a free-for-all, but knee-jerk responses will get you into trouble, and cause more damage to your brand than any customer or prospect.

Instead of spearheading a copyright war, Viacom would have been better served creating a social, interactive, sticky Web site as soon as YouTube and MySpace showed traction.[2] The branded content (TV shows) that appeared on YouTube could have been used to draw viewers back to Viacom's branded site. The company should have extended the experience around their content by adding insider conversations with celebrities and show creators, and show out-takes to their site. The vast user interactivity with Viacom's content illustrates how exceptional it is—and content is still king. Using content ownership to your advantage by drawing bigger audiences back to your brand is the way to win.

Online social behavior is a boon to entertainment companies if they can use it to build their brands and customer loyalty. It's not that copyright is irrelevant or that it should be ignored. Viacom and all content owners have the right to determine the use of their content and reap financial benefits from it. However, in a Webosphere that companies cannot control, *what is the best way to manage copyright?* This subject is much too big for this book, but companies need to determine how they are going to manage their content and how they are going to respond to unauthorized use of their content. It has become clear that smart marketers are collaborating to create and share content, partnering to share revenue, and encouraging users to interact and link to it. Viacom's lawsuit has done little to assuage user behavior because users enjoy the freedom to post what they like, and what they think others will like. The copyright lawsuit may help Viacom gain greater control over how their content is used, thereby restricting Google and other Web sites, but it won't help them win customers.

The distributed experience means that your content will be out there in unplanned ways. You do need to put resources behind monitoring what is happening with your brand. But more importantly, your response to rogue behavior should be similar to IBM's approach to the Linux open source community discussed in Chapter Three. Learn the rules of the environment, then make sure your interaction and responses fit in. You will have a better chance of having a positive impact. And don't forget the goal, establish a philosophy for how your content will attract customers, pull them to your Web site, and hold onto them for as long as possible.

Clear Focus, Clear Strategy

In this interactive, Live Web experience, marketers must establish a clear philosophy for how the vicinities on the Web will be monitored and managed (interacted with), for how content will be permeated with unique value (and the message you own), and for how marketers will create links in a chain that continuously brings viewers to their Web pages no matter where the branded content is first experienced. Whether it's TV ads, videos, informational papers, and even the product itself, users' first interaction maybe where you intended it or somewhere else, so make sure your content is designed to draw your audience back to you.

Your Live Web guiding philosophy will determine how flexible you are with your brand, and to what length you will go to own your message in the minds of your audience. Today companies can bid on *your* brand name to advertise *their* products online. Consumers can search on the terms "Burger King" and the top result is their local In-N-Out Burger. You must determine in advance what you will do with unexpected or undesired user interactions or competitor behaviors. *How can you turn those interactions into value-add?* Smart companies choose their battles carefully. Often, it is more important to allow users to experience your brand in their own way, and learn from their experiences rather than fight them in court.

Being flexible with your brand and marketing initiatives is a big part of becoming an authentic part of the Live Web. Building this type of flexibility into your marketing department, while at the same time staying focused and strategic about priorities, is complex. Start with the basics, such as bidding highest on your brand name for online ads and optimizing your Web site for superior organic search results. Then, set up marketing initiatives that meet specific objectives—ensuring all have a digital element. Encourage marketers to be open to outsider behavior, comments, and input. As you broaden your efforts to include social networking elements, make sure all levels of management are comfortable with the unexpected interactions, and willing to embrace these behaviors.

Smart marketers are also driving their companies to act with one voice. Often as a company's marketing efforts grow, areas of specialty develop. Before long, there are outside agencies and marketing departments for traditional advertising, online advertising, direct response, public relations, Web, promotions, and field sales marketing. Each develops a strategy and set of objectives. And more often than not, marketing is splintered. Companies miss out on the snowball effect of messages and activities that build together. Marketers talk of "integrated programs," but if programs need to be integrated, that means they were designed as stand-alone, separate activities—and that's where the trouble starts.

To make sense of and correlate marketing programs, marketers must have a clear focus and strategy that rises above the digital versus traditional marketing debate. Live Web elements should be an integral part of each marketing activity, but that doesn't mean all marketing should be online only. You choose the vehicle based on the objective. If you are trying to reach a local audience at drive time, your best solution is likely a billboard or radio ad. If your objective is the broadest reach possible, then your best bet is to place an ad with the American Idol television show.

Smith & Hawken, Patagonia, Williams-Sonoma, and Victoria's Secret can attest to the fact that catalogs drive up Web-site activity. Catalogs are one of the most effective opportunities to make an emotional appeal and build brand. Zappos.com, the online shoe company, and Kiras.com, the online candy company, both developed catalogs after they had started as online-only businesses.[3] Web-based companies have determined that ecommerce is efficient for purchasing but doesn't do much to attract customers. Catalogs, billboards, and trade magazine ads can be used to drive viewers online for more information, for a promotion, or for an event, while they brand and extend your message at the same time. Offline marketing still carries a big bang for the buck. Whether online or off, the Live Web demands marketing efforts from product development to billboards are designed to pull the audience in, interact, and engage them.

There is still the issue of communications clutter and audience overload. Consumers are learning to tune out banner ads, and they are often overwhelmed by the volume of email in their inbox. Breakout, provocative ideas are what work. Target, Adidas, and Clorox have run interactive ads on New York subway station walls. The ads draw people in to touch and learn. One Target ad changes scenery and drops snowflakes to a viewer's hand waving. An Adidas ad lights up when people walk by, then starts a shower of shoes that grows larger as the person moves around.[4] As mobile phones become more advanced in the U.S., we will be able to point and click our phones at an ad and receive all kinds of interesting, useful, or funny information.

The disruption marketers face is a new engagement model which requires social elements. Employees, prospects, and customers *expect* to participate and have a voice. Participation in brands is a straightforward expectation for students now coming out of college. It won't be long before they are the dominant consumers and business purchasers. Meeting their expectations for engagement requires a new kind of marketing. Marketing 2.0 is designed to get your audience to *engage* and *interact*—to get them involved. Insular companies fearful of giving outsiders (and employees) a voice are at a disadvantage as their competitors create extended communities and loyalty. The ability for your product, your content, and your message to attract, captivate, and hold your audience's attention is the marketing challenge of this age. And you have substantially more choices for how you can distribute your message, brand your product, and attract prospects—all of them designed to help you succeed.

There are so many marketing vehicles it is difficult to discuss them all in a single chapter. If there is one clear message this book offers its readers, it is that great marketing is based on a core, unique value, and that all areas of execution are about engaging your audience with that value. Smart marketers drive the marketing vehicles they deploy by seeping the same message across all forms of execution, and by maintaining a high level strategy that focuses creative and innovative concepts across all implementations. Focus and consistency make your brand and products meaningful to your audience. From their Web sites to their online and traditional advertising to their promotional events, the following companies hold to a clear voice, vision, and value.

Volcom	anti-establishment
Viking	tasteful lifestyle
Patagonia	passion for the environment

The fact that marketing messages are distributed across the Web with less control by marketers hasn't hurt the brands or the companies that own them. Instead, it pushes companies to be flexible, open, and interactive thereby creating stronger relationships with their customers, partners, and employees.

Your Web Site Still Rules

Today, customers are more likely to learn more about your products and brand from sources you don't control than from the ones that you do. This dilemma invites a two-pronged approach. Monitor and influence audience activity on the Web, and draw customers and prospects back to your arena. Corporate Web sites began as a place to put the product brochure online, and quickly evolved into a place of commerce. Many companies for the first time could communicate with and sell directly to their customers.

The Live Web disrupts the traditional, static Web-site model. The corporate Web site is quickly turning into a social environment, a shopping mall if you will, where people come to socialize, explore, shop, and be entertained. It is also a place where content can be uploaded or created, then pushed or pulled across the Web. Web sites are becoming flexible, organic systems that evolve and grow via the interactions and needs of users. A flat, uniform, unvaried Web site is now a relic of times past.

The corporate Web site offers the essential opportunity to interact, engage, and continuously brand your company. It can clarify your position in the marketplace, and give you a platform for authenticity and credibility. It is *the* place to market your company. And it is the quintessential place to listen to and talk to your audiences, as well as give them a voice. You can also give executives and employees a public voice. These types of freedoms may seem frightening at first. *What will employees say on their blog? What if customers complain? How do we control it?* Well, participation is more important than control. First, you need to establish how you will encourage and influence the message. Then, you should set basic rules for behavior (no bad language or graphic images, be respectful to others, etc.) in a social networking, blogging, or public discourse policy. Finally, you must open your eyes and ears and learn from what's going on. If no one's talking about your company or products, they aren't relevant. If there's lots of negative chatter, fix the problems. If one incorrect or negative post or comment has become viral, get on top of it, as Kryptonite should have done in the following example.

In September 2004, writer Phillip Torrone posted an article on Engadget.com stating that he had easily picked a Kryptonite Evolution 2000 U bike lock with a Bic ballpoint pen. There were one-hundred-and-eighty-eight reader comments following the article from Kryptonite customers both enraged at and supportive of the company. Included in the comments was a formal (a.k.a. bland) corporate response from Kryptonite, a unit of Ingersoll Rand.[5] They had missed a crucial opportunity to say, yes we are aware of the flaw in our product; this is what we will do to fix customer owned locks; and this is how we will solve the problem through our future product plans.

The Engadget post was picked up by the mainstream press and the negative flare up caused a sales downturn for Kryptonite that quarter. Kryptonite reversed its stance, created a voluntary lock exchange program, redesigned its lock, and replaced over four-hundred-thousand customer-owned locks for free. Without the editor's post on Engadget.com, the company may not have learned about their product's weakness (or done anything about it), and continued to put customer valuables at risk, diminishing years of built up trust. Had Kryptonite's Web site hosted social engagement, they would have learned of the issue earlier and been able to respond better. Customers would have been more likely to respond with their concerns directly to the company.

Engaging and interacting with your audience is what makes a good company great in the age of engage. Remaining insular and closing your eyes to the Live Web doesn't mean all of this consumer behavior will go away. It will just happen somewhere you are not. Competitors or start-ups will gain an advantage as they choose to be more open, interactive, and engaging, drawing larger and more loyal audiences.

It's interesting to see how Volcom, a relatively young company, has grown so quickly, outpacing its biggest rival Quiksilver, Inc. To learn how they are doing this, check out the Volcom.com Web site. If you shudder when you see the images, you are not a prospect for this company's clothing line. Interestingly, if you take a moment on the site, you will find it is difficult to tell they sell a product. They are talking to their audience and only their audience, young, edgy, surfers, skateboarders, snowboarders—well, you know the type. Volcom's unique value is inherent in their site which is designed to create a community around their antiestablishment creed. The Web site is designed to have people opt in and become a part, a player. Volcom has turned podcasts into rich, social experiences as well as entertainment and branding events. *Volcasts*, as they call them, cover surfing, skateboarding, snowboarding, girls, and music. Featuring live moments and events, the Volcasts at the same time offer a sense of voyeurism. *You are now experiencing what we experienced and love. You should have been there.* The audience is given a sense of the company, its authenticity, and community. The Web site is one continuous branding event.

Dell is also using its Web site to clean up the company's image as a provider of impersonal and poor customer service. On its IdeaStorm site, customers are invited to offer input, commentary, voting (viewers vote for the ideas they like best), and discussion. It is at the same time social and educational for all involved. Dell is also offering customers insight into future products. This is a gutsy change for a highly insular company. So far the response has been good with over forty-five-hundred customer ideas provided, and over three-hundred-thousand votes, as of this writing.

Elements of social networking on your Web site enable employees, prospects, or customers to interact with each other, and learn more about each other. They have the opportunity to share thoughts and ideas, images, and video. The company can share more about its executives, employees, products, problems, and processes to offer outsiders insight. As long as you know customers are out there talking about you, *why not move the conversation home—for everyone to see? Wouldn't that make it easier to incorporate user feedback quickly?* It can be implemented through a comments section where customers can provide their thoughts, ideas, issues, and concerns. It's time to move beyond the conventional bulletin board with its linear question and answer format, and incorporate blogs, podcasts, comments, and social spaces where customers can talk to each other and relate to each other, and talk to and relate to your employees.

Corporate Web sites or corporate-sponsored Web sites such as Proctor & Gamble's Capessa.com are the starting points for creating an open, authentic, social environment. Web 2.0-savvy companies add del.icio.us or Technorati tags and voting to articles and product descriptions. They add comments sections to their blogs. They syndicate (using RSS) much of the material that goes on their Web site including blogs, podcasts, videos, and reports. Smart marketers are making their companies part of the conversations inherent in the marketplace, and allowing the marketplace to choose what content will become part of the Live Web conversation. They are also using Web sites to create innovative platforms for user engagement.

A lot can be said for Nike's response to getting shut out of the 2006 World Cup Soccer advertising. Adidas won the rights to be the only sports marketer—and this is no small win. World Cup Soccer draws a larger audience than the Olympics or the Super Bowl. But getting shut out of traditional advertising may have been the best thing that could have happened to Nike. Their out-of-the-box thinking drove them to link up with Google and set up the first social networking site for soccer fans, Joga.com.[6] Using the Web site, they could take advantage of the increased soccer mindshare during the competition, yet have a long-lasting forum to develop a relationship with and hold on to young customers.

The result of social interactions on your Web site is often customer loyalty, and loyalty creates a contract between you and your customer. It keeps the customer coming back. *Why not give points to people who visit your Web site?* If they watch a demo, listen to a new product presentation, chat online with a sales rep, or a number of other activities, they could earn points. If they provide their email address or business address and opt-in to receive communications, surveys, or other marketing materials they could earn more points. Those points would add up to goodies they could win, such as free maintenance for a month, a free copy or sample, a great new business book, or something else your audience might be interested in.

Although you define and create your brand, you have to be flexible in allowing your audience to interact with it. Use your Web site as the definitive authority on what you stand for and what makes your company unique, while at the same time substantiating your brand and making your company vision and story more believable. As your marketing message trickles through a variety of marketing vehicles ensure home base is a place your audience will want to end up. Your Web site is the one place you can rely on to continually brand and maintain your differentiator. Consumers opt in. They participate by using your product. They get involved beyond the purchase. The more you can create a live, social environment that hugs these customers, the better.

The opportunity to reach and delight customers seems endless. If you continue to build trust and delight your customer, the relationship grows. And in today's Live-Web world, you can take advantage of that contract to increase word-of-mouth from your loyal customers, and turn them into advocates.

Social Spaces and User Interactivity

The elements of social networking provide a new level in which to engage the customer. It gives them a reason to stay on your Web site versus spending their time on Yahoo! or YouTube. *Do you have the type of product that is conducive to customers submitting their own videos using it? Could your customers submit audio stories of their experiences?* There are several options today for adding social functions to your Web site. There are companies that will host the service for you and companies that offer software tools you can install and manage, including Reality Digital, Ning, Small World Labs, KickApps, and IBM's Lotus Connections. Along with all of the good social interactivity brings, you will also experience negative behavior, and it is important to deal openly with these actions. Allowing all perspectives is authentic and makes your company more believable. Responding in a timely manner to issues that are raised, shows your customers how invested you are in them.

Social networking can be implemented on internal-use-only intranets using LinkedIn-style personal pages which would add social elements for employees. LinkedIn is a business networking site where users post their resume with links to their blogs and Web sites, recommendations from colleagues, lists of interests, awards, associations, and people in their network. This type of personal space allows employees to learn more about the people they work with. If you make some of the information public, it can also help customers learn more about who they are dealing with.

LinkedIn-style social pages could significantly enhance a customer service organization. Customer service has one of the biggest impacts on a customer's opinion of a company. Yet, when we talk to or chat with a service rep, we know nothing about them. A page with their picture, information about their tenure at the company, their personal expertise, and even some of their personal thoughts could enhance the relationship. Too many companies keep up an impersonal, distant façade, which is most unengaging. Their customer service goal is to solve the problem and get the customer off the phone as fast as humanly possible. The opportunity for trust, credibility, and loyalty is missed. Allowing customers to get to know employees, putting a face on developers, finance people, and support people can completely change interactions. Simple, inconsequential talks can build relationships, and that builds trust and loyalty, as well as a better return on your marketing, as IBM learned.

With the goal of attracting and converting leads in the mid-sized business market, IBM worked with its resellers to generate leads through advertising, and by offering a more personal service when responding to questions from prospects. IBM set up a micro Web site as the landing page for the ads, so that when prospects responded they were sent only to select service reps. These select reps were given a video camera on their desktops so that prospects that logged on to chat could see who they were speaking with. Lead-to-sale results were four times higher than previous IBM lead-generation campaigns.[7]

If your only goal is to get a prospect to purchase, you've missed the opportunity for long-term engagement and a loyal relationship. The Web 2.0 technology that makes up the Live Web gives every company the opportunity to engage customers. Social elements enhance interactivity, but they also create context. They give greater meaning to your core value. Most companies are accustomed to providing the entire context around their products and company. When you let go of some of that control, the marketplace offers a broader set of ideas and actions than any company can provide on its own. Proctor & Gamble management has pushed employees to be more open and to actually embrace outside ideas in its "proudly found elsewhere" model for doing business.[8] The company is now flexible with its brands, where once it controlled their use with an iron fist.

Frito-Lay has also embraced outsider creativity. In planning its marketing for the 2007 Super Bowl, Frito-Lay marketing executives jumped into the Live Web with both feet. Their strategy was to use the Live Web to reinvent the marketing around Doritos, a thirty-year-old snack-food brand. Their objective was an authentic ad campaign, and at the same time to learn more about their brand, consumer, and product experience. Their planning led them to three profound consumer truths: *self-expression, independence,* and *belonging.* These same truths drive the Live Web. The marketing team, which included several outside agencies, created the Crash the Super Bowl promotion around these beliefs. A Web site was set up and consumers were invited to produce their own thirty-second Doritos commercial. The creators of the five best submissions would be invited to the Super Bowl, and the winner would find out live when their commercial aired.[9]

The Web site received fifty submissions and 2 million visitors in the first week, far above anyone's expectations. There were social aspects to the site enabling viewers to talk to each other about the ads that had been submitted. A total of one-thousand-and-seventy commercials were submitted, and millions of online conversations logged. In the end, two commercials were aired, *Checkout Girl* and *Live the Flavor*. The latter cost just $12.79 to produce. Both commercials were designed and produced by amateurs with no advertising experience, just a passion for the product. *Checkout Girl* has been viewed over three-hundred-and-eighty-thousand times on YouTube and appears on countless other video Web sites. *Live the Flavor* has been viewed over 1.4 million times on YouTube. The promotion illustrates the passion and perspective customers bring to your product, as well as how effective it can be to combine digital and traditional marketing goals. The combination of a highly engaging contest with a Super Bowl placement, which gives the ad extraordinarily broad reach, was provocative enough to draw 350 million press impressions including mainstream news publications and TV news programs.

Stephen Colbert, of Comedy Central's The Colbert Report (a political satire), certainly understands how to engage his audience. Beyond his blog on colbertnation.com, Colbert launched a highly successful video promotion on YouTube, the *Green Screen Challenge*. To launch the promotion, Colbert shot video of himself jumping about with a lightsaber in front of a green screen so that fans could easily edit the video in any way they chose, then upload it to YouTube. Not only were hundreds of videos produced and uploaded, each received thousands (or hundreds of thousands) of views. The best were chosen by Colbert and aired on his cable television show. You can encourage interactions by injecting your own fun and humor. Best Buy's Geek Squad is one of the only technical service organizations that illustrates they are working hard and having fun at the same time. You can't miss the *Men in Black* style uniform and language—they are on a mission.

As marketers, it is the unexpected that frightens and delights us. No one wants bad news to go viral. But today companies are judged more on their response than on the original problem. FedEx and Kryptonite are now well aware of this. The marketers at Frito-Lay took a risk putting their product and brand out there for consumers to play with. The result taught them more about what people love about Doritos than any customer survey or focus group. The Live Web gives companies the opportunity to learn more about their products and the market's perspective of their company, invaluable information that shouldn't be ignored.

Distribute Your Brand Experience

If you start with a strategy that defines one clear value, then drive that value across all marketing mediums, even with different implementations, you can expect your target audience to remember your brand, message, and positioning. The distributed experience is about connecting the dots between these different audience experiences through a consistent style, tone, and message. It is also about incorporating an interactive element that keeps your audience engaged and associated with your company through online forums. Whether the marketing tactics or ads are a brief eight-second spot during a user-generated Web TV episode, or a two-minute video uploaded to YouTube, the consistency will help your audience see and feel the connection.

What do you want your brand experience to be? How should customers feel or respond to your marketing? Determine how you can execute against your objectives with high impact across marketing vehicles, while supporting one high-level value. Whether it's a five-word link ad, thirty-second commercial, two-minute video, or a CEO blog, the company differentiator, value, or passion needs to shine through. Beyond the vehicles you choose to push your message, determine in advance which vicinities on the Live Web your audience is likely to receive your message. *How can you infiltrate these communities and influence the message?* Successfully distributing a connected message can be as simple as adding your Web site link to your widget or ensuring your logo is associated with all of your content as it moves around the Web. It is much more complex in companies with multiple products, multiple messages, and no one overriding principle guiding all execution.

Complexity is inherent when multiple groups in a company are approaching the market from different perspectives. Competing messages confuse audiences. Clear focus and consistency need to underlie all creative execution.

It's not enough to push your message out through every marketing vehicle you can afford. Great creative and a provocative idea are needed to capture the minds of your audience. Whether it's an online ad, viral video, email marketing campaign, direct mail, or billboard, a great idea or original creative execution wins. Creative concepts can make audiences think, laugh, and act. As companies are pushed to reinvent their Web sites, delve into video, and try out immersive 3D environments such as Second Life, they have to determine how to consistently implement their strategy, while executing with creative and innovative programs.

Capturing the attention of your target audience when they are continuously over-marketed to, and have learned to tune out ads, takes a big idea. Magic happens when a creative idea aligns with your strategy, unique value, and customer. Break-out, provocative ideas will work for companies that historically have been conservative. Burger King's advertising agency overcame a long run of unimaginative ads when it produced the interactive and viral Subservient Chicken (www.subservientchicken.com) campaign. Users of the Web site type in commands to make a man in a chicken suit jump, sit, watch TV, stand on his head, and well, almost anything they can think of. Before a user types in the first command, they see the message, *chicken anyway you want it*. The Web site received 14 million unique visitors over a year, and people still visit the site two years later.[10]

Although successful at breaking through and getting consumers to interact, the campaign fell down at the point where viewers clicked on the link to Burger King's corporate Web site—no special landing page was set up to continue the conversation or inform the viewer. The corporate Web site does nothing to promote Burger King's chicken sandwiches or any other product. It doesn't continue to entice or interact with the audience—what a mistake.

The reality is that a great deal of advertising is poorly conceived and executed, and often marketing programs don't build to a whole greater than its parts. It's common for large companies to lose focus. Small companies complain they don't have enough resources. Consumers are inundated daily with ads that offer no unique value, core belief, story, or engagement for the product being marketed. Business purchasers attend trade shows and listen to vendor pitches, then when they return to their offices, they have to determine how the product fits their need, or business perspective, or view of the marketplace. When the passion, the product, and the message don't align, customers have to work too hard to determine if they want your product.

Subservient Chicken falls under the *viral* marketing umbrella. Viral campaigns can instantaneously reach millions of viewers, an effect of the highly social, Live Web. Hundreds of millions of conversations are happening in real-time, and the idea is to get people talking about your company, product, or marketing. Yet, it's not enough to produce a successful viral campaign or user-generated video contest, you must align these provocative ideas with your Web site, paid search ads, banner ads, etc. in terms of tone, style, and overall message in order to gain a cumulative effect.

Give Them Something to Talk About

Ask yourself this *Is your product interesting enough that other people will want to talk about it? Does it surprise, delight, and deliver on its promise?* If the answer is yes, *what are you doing to ensure others are talking?* If the answer is no, *what can you do to create cachet?*

Buzz, also known as word-of-mouth marketing, won't come from a great ad campaign, direct mail, or brochure. Buzz is invisible, but that doesn't mean you can't manage or influence it. *Buzz* is essentially what people are saying about your product at any point in time. That can be good, and it can be bad. When marketers talk about buzz, they mean the positive, cumulative effect of people talking about your product, recommending it, and creating excitement around it.

An entire industry has spawned around buzz. As evidenced by the word-of-mouth (WOM) marketing field, its association WOMMA, and the number of new WOM companies, the generation of good gossip is becoming good business. Word-of-mouth is verbal buzz but it can be driven by visual elements such as video, images, or product itself. Video and email campaigns designed to be forwarded or linked to are most often called *viral* marketing. Yet, the industry doesn't know what makes a specific campaign go viral, or why it is forwarded to thousands, hundreds of thousands, or millions of people. Nor do they currently have the metrics to determine if a viral campaign is successful. It will be difficult to create metrics until enough campaigns are produced and measured in order to evaluate comparisons and averages.

How does buzz work? Well, real people have to use your product in order to talk about it. So, the idea is to engage customers by getting product into their hands. These can be free copies to luminaries, press, and target customers. Software companies often offer free software downloads for a trial period. Emanuel Rosen in his book, *The Anatomy of Buzz*, states that Tom Peters and Bob Waterman sent out fifteen-thousand copies of a one-hundred-and-twenty-five-page summary of their book *In Search of Excellence* prior to its launch. The book sold 1.5 million copies in hardcover. Most authors seed the market with just two-hundred to three-hundred copies of a pre-print version of their book, and the average business book sells just twenty-five thousand copies. Many companies already provide free samples of their product to target groups. The Tom Peters example is designed to make you think differently about this type of program. Not only is the free sample a core marketing strategy, it defines the openness and assuredness the company has with their product. Go big. You want to think beyond your traditional target groups—think breadth and depth. Buzz doesn't often jump beyond a specific group of individuals. You have to seed as many different types of groups as possible.

There are companies designed specifically around the concept of buzz. Buzz marketing organizations attract and manage a community of people willing to test products, interact on Web sites, or read books, and then actively talk about the products to their friends, on their blogs, or on other Web sites (such as commenting on a book on Amazon). In this way, it is possible to help catalyze grassroots, early adopter behavior, as long as your product is interesting and delightful.[11] Consumers are still surprised and delighted by products that work easily and continuously, by great customer service, and by a product or service that solves exactly their problem, or meets their specific need. When a product delights, consumers engage with the product and talk about it, and buy aftermarket functions. They join clubs, user groups, and social sites specific to the product. Without delightful and marketable features, buzz won't take hold.

Thanks to YouTube and MySpace, viral video has become a new way to spread an idea or create buzz. It is so simple to share a video these days, that it makes sense to use this tactic for almost any product. The video itself needs to surprise, delight, fascinate, or inform. It must be superior in one of these areas so that people are compelled to pass it along or talk about it. Some of the most popular viral videos have been corporate ads including Smirnoff's "Tea Partay," Burger King's "Subservient Chicken," and Folgers "Happy Mornings." Honda's two-minute "Cog" video employs a real-life domino-effect using all Honda parts. It's fascinating to watch and has garnered hundreds of thousands of views on YouTube and several other sites. Soon after the video aired on TV and online, visits to Honda's Web site quadrupled, and calls to Honda's information center tripled.[12]

Another way to create buzz or viral marketing is with interactive email. An example of a huge email marketing success was Career-Builder.com's Monk-e-mail which allowed people to create their own animated cartoon chimpanzees who deliver verbal messages to recipients. The email was fun, and clearly aligned with CareerBuilder's business, voice, strategy, and tone. It directed customers to a great Web site that was simple to navigate. (You can find it at www.careerbuilder.com/monk-e-mail/.) And so many people could relate to being frustrated with the people they work with (the monkeys) that their viral behavior generated over 60 million email cards.[13]

Ad agencies promote their ability to build viral campaigns like CareerBuilder.com's Monkey-e-mail or OfficeMax's Elf Yourself campaign. And marketing companies like BzzAgent develop their own communities of consumers that are paid to create buzz around a new product or service. Their job is to catalyze word-of-mouth—but it's not that simple. It takes the unexpected, provocative, or just plain fun program to go viral. It takes an unexpected, delightful, and most importantly, useful product to create real word-of-mouth. You can't manufacture buzz if there's nothing to buzz about, and flaws in your product will be raised publicly by those very same buzz agents. So heading down the path of viral doesn't make any sense unless you've done your job with the core product and core value first.

Something that is new, unusual, or free is more likely to create excitement, and give people a reason to talk. Constantly creating new products, features, or services, and developing valuable items to give away, needs to be a core business strategy. That way you have the opportunity to keep the conversation going, and create new spikes in your buzz campaign. Ryanair does this so well. Having reorganized in

1990 to become Europe's first low-fare airline following the model set by Southwest Airlines, Ryanair chose to supercharge its model in 2000 with its Web site and novel approach to air travel.

Ryanair's no-frills seats are extraordinarily cheap—or even given away free—charging customers only for taxes and fees. (Free airline seats! Now that's something to talk about.) Checked baggage, snacks, drinks, and any other extras come with a charge. Ryanair's Web-centric model enables the company to sell ninety-eight-percent of its tickets online and offer a host of services including insurance, hotel bookings, car rentals, gift vouchers, and online check-in.[14] Because they've broadened their revenue model beyond tickets, they manage to soak in changes in the price of gasoline without passing on gas surcharges to the customer. And by making their airline a Web business (their software interface to the customer), the company can quickly and easily innovate, and ad services and features at a minimal cost. They've certainly given the market something to talk about—and it shows. Their customer base has grown from 7 million in 2000 to 42.5 million in 2006, while most other airlines have struggled.

Create Push and Pull

Drawing audiences to your Web site is fundamental. Creating pull where *your audience* distributes your content and message *for you* is pure Marketing 2.0, and widget marketing is the newest pull vehicle. Widgets are becoming a bigger part of the distributed-content phenomenon. They offer an option for syndicating information without requiring a reader (separate Web page). The widget appears right on a desktop, or inside a blog or Web site. JC Penney uses a widget to continuously update retail content and deals for its highly-engaged customers.[15] NBC Universal is enabling Web-site owners and bloggers to post a widget that receives NBC programming snippets.[16] This type of branded syndication is a great way to constantly remind customers of your value, as well as keep your brand top-of-mind.

Bitty Browser and Yahoo!'s MyBlogLog are widgets with interesting functionality. Bitty Browser allows users to install a fully-functional mini browser on their Web site. Similar to picture-in-picture on TV sets, the micro browser enables another Web site to be live within your Web site. The MyBlogLog widget lists the photos and online names of readers as they visit your blog. Yahoo, Google, and Mozilla (Firefox) offer hundreds of widgets so users can display stock tickers, weather, and the date and time on their computer desktop. Yahoo's widgets put users one click away from Yahoo's Web site where they can get more information.

Widgets are a unique way for companies to distribute content. They are interesting, fun, and entertaining, but more than that, widgets extend branding and message in a viral format. Companies can provide a product demo, product updates, or news information in a widget, the more viewers that like the widget, the ever-increasing number of Web sites that will embed it for additional viewers to see. Even better, widgets are becoming two-way. RateItAll, a social network for online reviews and opinions, offers a rating widget. Post the rating widget on your blog, and users can input their rating and send it in.[17]

Whether you are creating push or pull for your content, Marketing 2.0 drives us to think more clearly about how we package content into small, movable, flexible chunks. Syndicating your content via RSS feeds works, but it's best to separate feeds by clear categories, such as customer stories, input and ideas, technical data, and what's new. There is so much information and entertainment on the Web that small, digestible nuggets are the best format. You also want to market your feeds by reminding customers where to sign up on your Web site, in your newsletter, and through other marketing programs, and by making sure your feeds are packaged and titled so they can be listed on Blogwise, Feedshot, Newsgator, Yahoo, and Google. To gain the most advantage from your RSS feeds, make sure the links included in feeds are accurate, and send readers to the correct Web page. Continually assess your syndicated content for consistency of message, in-depth knowledge, and its ability to entice readers back to your Web site. Widgets and RSS help you to think differently about the Web and how you communicate with your audiences. You are no longer able to write content once, then update it in a year. To keep audiences engaged, you must have on-staff writers that are working in real-time. Daily updates of news and information, and monitoring user responses draws customers back on a regular basis. When you set up a podcast, access executives, managers, and experts in the company, and interview knowledgeable guests to broaden the perspective on your differentiation and message. Better yet, take your podcast on the road to tradeshows and company events—make it an enjoyable, informative, and engaging experience. Let your audience see inside your company, experience the personalities of executives and employees, and feel more a part of the world you have created.

The Laws of Attraction

The Live Web challenges every company to live and breath digital. Traditional marketing should drive your audience to interact with your Web site. Print ads, direct response, and billboards must be part of the same strategy and execution used for online campaigns. Marketing programs should feel like a conversation with your target audience, where you talk to consumers in a way they are now accustomed, and give consumers a way to talk to others about you. There are several options for enabling consumers to interact with your marketing. They can answer a question, figure out a riddle, or play a game. Marketing should be provocative, unexpected, and interesting. The interactivity and social bent of the Internet have driven up our expectations for how marketers must execute.

And we are seeing firsthand how social and interactive elements are affecting the business of advertising. Big marketers are extending their reach by setting up branded content sites to draw audiences to their message, and in most cases to create community around subjects broader than their product lines. Proctor & Gamble's Capessa.com, Nike's Joga.com, Anheuser-Busch's Bud.tv, and General Motor's sponsored TV.com are a few of the corporate social and entertainment sites. Most companies can't afford to fund a separate entertainment and social Web site, yet they can use their corporate Web site to develop and incorporate content beyond their typical product information in order to position the company as a trusted partner and subject authority.

Yet, you still have to generate leads for your product or service. If you were an early participant in online advertising and paid search, you were able to pay exceptionally cheap prices for the best Web-site banner positions and keywords. Paid search is all about keywords. You bid on specific keywords you think your audience will use when searching to find a product or service like yours. Today, competition for keywords has exploded, and online advertising is no longer cheap. It's now critical to deploy a well-thought-through strategy that can be tested and implemented online, then driven across offline marketing vehicles. It is essential to think differently about online marketing. Thirty-second or sixty-second spots don't work as well in the online arena as they do on TV. Think short bites or moments for Web ads, or longer, more provocative pieces for viewing on YouTube. Find your way inside content through collaboration—become a part of a Web-TV program. Some of the best examples of content integration come from Reality TV advertising such as the Ford ads starring the American Idol contestants, or the company-specific tasks on The Apprentice. Today, you have to find a way to sell a big message through small, distributed nuggets.[18]

And while you're mastering this model, you need to adapt to the new process for evaluating and purchasing ad space. The fundamental business for media buying has changed. Specifically, the volume of online ads and Web sites that accept ads has generated a new model for buying and selling ad space. You can choose a specific online publisher and pay them directly to appear on their Web site, mirroring the traditional media buy used for TV. You can also become part of an *ad network*—a semi-automated system that purchases ad space based on the requirements of the advertiser. In this environment you work with the ad network's account manager to define a strategy, and then she makes the media buy through the ad network system which evaluates the member Web sites in their community based on your guidelines.

You can also use a fully-automated ad network, also called an *ad exchange*—which is essentially, an Ebay-style auction for ads. There are dozens of ad networks including 24/7 Real Media, Advertising.com, DoubleClick, Value Click, Burst!, Collective Media, Federated Media, Casale Media, and Tribal Fusion. Google, Yahoo!, and MSN offer ad networks, too. With most services, you don't actually know which Web sites your ads will appear, but more transparency is coming to ad networks and a deeper level of detail will come too. Currently, you can define the types of Web sites where you want your ads to appear, and the network chooses the actual sites the ad appears on. More transparency will allow you to restrict certain ads from appearing near yours, determine the time of day your ads appear, or choose exact placement on a specific Web site.

There is still a great deal marketers can learn from online advertising. Keyword research will teach you about the vernacular of your audience. It will help you think more about what makes your product unique and what words in common use apply to that value. One of the exceptional values of online advertising is that you can cost-effectively, quickly, and continually test multiple creative executions and keywords to determine which results in the intended response (click through rate, click to purchase, etc.). Analytics tools from Google and Yahoo, as well as third-parties give you all of the information you need. You can also test different landing page designs to see which draws the best response. When you identify the creative in your online campaign that works best, you can transfer that learning to your print or television ad campaigns, as both print and TV advertising take longer to evaluate, and you have to make assumptions about who is actually viewing the ad.

Aggressive marketers are always looking for successful formats to attract larger audiences to their brand, products, and Web site, and hold onto them. One of the well-established Marketing 2.0 tools used to do this is email marketing. *Email marketing* is about customers opting in to get your message. Customers tell you they are ready and willing to listen to you, providing you the opportunity to mail them offers or educational information. Developing, owning, and managing your list of prospects is an essential element of direct response which includes email marketing, direct mail, or catalogs. When customers and prospects have opted-in to be on your list, they have opened their inbox to you and said, "Okay, send me something interesting and I will read it." With regular communication you are much more likely to reach that customer when they are ready to buy. Annoy your audience with too much email or the wrong type of offers, or worse, email people who do not wish to hear from you, and you will only serve to damage your image and relationships. (It's a good idea to ask customers how often they would like to be contacted.)

Make sure if your email offer links to a Web site, you are linking them to a coherent next step. Email marketing allows you to be provocative, engaging, or just plain helpful. If you can get your target audience to click on a link, don't waste this opportunity. Just like a good host, let them know you were expecting them, and make sure each new friend is happy she chose to come to your home.

Target Online Behavior

The great thing about email marketing and direct mail tied to your Web site is that you can track the response rate *and* what the customer does next. If implemented correctly, you can track email opens and forwards, and clicks to your Web site from the link in the email. You can use an email marketing agency or an automated online service such as *i*Contact or Constant Contact. With email marketing, you not only know how many people respond as a percentage of your total list, you know what interested them, what they clicked on next, and how long they stayed on your site, or any specific page. You can track the same user's activities each time they enter your site giving you a better picture of that person, then you can determine how to market to them better. All of this information can be stored in a database and evaluated, helping you to hone your marketing process and get better results each time. Amazon has led this type of customer targeting. Their suggestions list and "other users chose these items" display is based on previous viewing and purchasing behaviors (yours as wells as other customers). Amazon displays these tools as a service, but the intent is to get consumers to purchase more products.

This type of customer-list optimization and targeted advertising is called *behavioral targeting* (BT). Every click on the Web can be tracked. Companies that deploy BT generally maintain information on individual behavior that occurs on their Web site. Amazon, eBay, Overstock. com, Ice.com, and Delightful Deliveries track your online behavior in order to make timely and useful suggestions or offers in ads.[19] Either previous visits or the search term used to reach the site can be used to drive which offer a user receives, say, a five-percent discount or free shipping. Microsoft uses BT to determine which third-party ads appear for a specific user based on his previous clicks.[20] Optimizing advertising, offers, and promotions to individuals is engaging.

It is possible to know so much about consumers that it feels like an invasion of their privacy—a line you don't want to cross. When eBay rolled out its custom ad system, the company added a new preference called AdChoice in the account management section of the site. AdChoice enables the user to allow or disallow eBay from using their personal information and online behavior to target ads to them. Users can even change their preferences right from an ad that has been served to them. Allowing users to manage their privacy level is a smart way to establish trust and loyalty.

The goal of BT is to gather, filter, and analyze a customer's data so that better, more meaningful, and useful ads can be targeted to that customer. Beyond that, BT provides an extraordinary learning opportunity for companies with regard to their customers.

New Worlds, Virtual Worlds

Engaging marketing starts on your Web site. It becomes a distributed experience through provocative ads, email, and viral campaigns. It may also lead you to other worlds. Immersive 3D sites such as Second Life and Doppelganger are currently hangouts for all types of businesses and consumers. Unlike Club Penguin and Nicktropolis which are brand-owned, fully-designed sites (targeted to kids), Second Life attracts physical world companies which set up shop and conduct business in the virtual world. Companies use fairly rich tools to create avatars (people), clothing, vehicles, environments, terrain, buildings, offices, and experiences. This user-generated content isn't simply for view and comment like MySpace or YouTube. These 3D interpretations create an interactive, entertaining, and informative experience. Companies launch products, hold events, talk to customers, and sell product (virtual and real) in virtual worlds.

Early experiences indicate that virtual worlds are a great place to hold company training sessions, collaborate with distant employees or partners, or entertain through movies or stage shows. Rivers Run Deep Ltd. and The Electric Sheep Company, among many others, build 3D content for companies that don't have the technical resources in house. The experience you create will represent your brand, and needs to be consistent and high quality. Or, on the other hand, if you want to be inconsistent—if you want to try on a *new* image (and begin the process to reinvent your marketing)—this may just be the place to do it.

As compute power increases while computer costs continue to decline, it's not difficult to imagine that most online experiences will become 3D, rich in quality and nearly realistic. Today, there are companies that provide complete 3D animated commercials where the product looks real—even better than real. When the product is recreated using software, the boundaries of what you can do in a commercial are broadened exponentially. You can make a product jump through hoops, literally. Immersive 3D whether in a virtual world, traditional Web site, or TV ad can create an unexpected and delightful experience that engages your target audience.

Virtual worlds are growing in number and growing their audiences quickly. However, from a *pure marketing or branding perspective*, it is currently unclear what participating in Second Life returns its big brand patrons including Coke, IBM, Calvin Klein, Adidas, or Toyota. Virtual worlds demand social and entertainment elements from the companies doing business there. Grassroots virtual companies—built originally as virtual-world entities—have seen an advantage and good success drawing crowds, over the traditional brands that have set up shop. Phat Cat's Jazzy Blue Lounge, a business originally created as an entity in Second Life, has been more tuned in to the interactions and formats that fit the community. Large corporations can afford to play around in this environment while determining how to get the best return. They have also found great benefit in using virtual worlds for enhanced internal interactions between people who otherwise would not see each other. It is definitely a marketing vehicle to watch. Virtual worlds and their participants will evolve quickly, and 3D avatars and interactive ads will eventually become standard elements of traditional Web worlds. This is one part of the new marketing paradigm that will be fun to see evolve.

You may be surprised by the creativity that can be found in your audience. Virtual worlds are an example of Web sites created in whole by user-generated content. The Web's most visited social sites—YouTube, MySpace, Digg, and Facebook—derive their existence and growth from user-generated content. These Web communities are platforms, and *all* of the content is created by a subset of the customers.[21] Today's consumer clearly wants a voice and to express their individual creativity. They also want to belong, or associate with a group to experience other people's expressions. User-generated doesn't diminish corporate-generated, but it does change the rules to customer engagement.

Overall, the intimate relationship companies have with their customers can have a huge impact on marketing. Web sites welcome customers by name, and suggest items based on what the customer previously purchased. Promotional emails arrive in a personal inbox. Customers invite companies into their homes and lives each day just by turning on the TV, PC, or cellphone. This intimacy suggests a level of trust the customer has put in the company. It also suggests a compelling and mutual relationship since customers now have the power of choice—whether or not to let you in. If treated with respect, this intimacy and mutual relationship gives marketers a much deeper platform in which they can engage their audience.

The marketing vehicles the Live Web has spawned create new challenges and big rewards. Companies will need to be flexible with their brands and open to free-flowing interactions with audiences. Marketers must ensure all product and brand initiatives and marketing programs communicate as one voice, consistent, yet creative. Success will be determined by the ability to choose the right marketing vehicles, distribute the message strategically, and deploy digital elements that interact with and engage audiences.

It is more important now than ever before to define your differentiating value based on real competencies, and to develop your vision, express your creed, and engage your audience to take them on a journey with you. This is a new era—Marketing 2.0 and the age of engage. It is a time to be open, authentic, and interactive. Engage your audience, and you and your business venture will succeed.

8

SITTING ON A ROCKET

MARKETING IS A CALLING TO BE A
CHANGE AGENT.

It is the marketer's job to change perspective, change markets, and change perceptions. By doing this, marketers can change the companies in which they work. The Live Web has created a new adventure by reinventing marketing. It is now easier than ever before to reach out and listen, learn, interact, and engage. The dynamics created by wikis, blogs, voting systems, buzz marketing, video, and virtual worlds can rocket your product to new heights. This is a pivotal time for marketers. The door is open to be entrepreneurial in spirit and behavior, even in a large company. The age of engage is about the extraordinary impact individuals, social groups, and market behavior has on a company's success—that puts marketing in a position of leadership. All you have to do is take the reins.

Your job is to think outside the box, defy conventional wisdom. Just about anyone can be creative. Being creative doesn't exactly mean being the one to create a completely original concept or technology, as engineers do in pure research labs, such as the famed Xerox PARC where Steve Jobs recognized the value in software work of some of the engineers there. Creativity is often about applying what has already been done in a unique or innovative way to the project at hand. Most often, that involves stealing. Yes, stealing. Lifting a good idea from another facet of life or a completely different industry and evolving it to meet your needs. Steve Jobs "lifted" the ideas he saw at Xerox PARC and implemented them in the Macintosh user interface. If you can't find an original or unexpected approach to your program, look at what companies in other industries are doing to see what might fit.

As consumers, we now have the ability to easily communicate and interact with strangers thousands or tens of thousands of miles away. We can do it passively or actively. In time, we won't differentiate where and how we communicate, whether it is on our computers, TV screens, mobile phones, computer games, or inside virtual worlds. Information and access will be seamless. For marketers this is fuel to feed a rocket. The ability to target individuals and their specific interests at any point or any place in which they choose to get online (of which they will be most of the time) will enhance branding. By using the tools available today and being ready for the new tools and platforms coming soon, you will be able to kick-start the fundamental power you already have. Web 2.0 and 3.0 technologies unleash the veracity of unique value, unexpected offers, compelling stories, and products that delight.

Gathering Fuel

The role of marketing is to know competitors, customers, and trends in the market. On top of that, marketers must have a deep understanding of their own company's products, technologies, and competencies. No other group or organization inside a company has the same breadth and depth, except for top management. Marketers must be Sherlock Holmes, J.K. Rowlings, and Stephen Hawking all rolled up into one.

As a great detective you need to dig deeper and ask more questions. Find out what your customers or your competitor's customers are saying about products in your market. *What do customers like? What are they complaining about?* Instead of formal meetings with your customer in his conference room or in yours, observe exactly how your product is being used. Talk to the people who are using it, and ask them

what they like best and what they like least, what project they're using the product for, what competitive products they use or have used,
and what they like best about those. Ask customers or prospects what's
happening in their industry, and talk to the people who won't buy your
product and understand what they are using and why.

The creative mind steals ideas from all parts of life, and develops
a good imagination of what could be. By tracking other company's
marketing activities through *AdAge, AdWeek, AdRants* and hundreds
of marketing Web sites and blogs, you will assess the good and bad
of what other people do and that will spark ideas. This is a time to
be curious about everything, to troll the Web for interesting sites and
behavior, or to use StumbleUpon or Cool Site of the Day to give you
ideas. Monitor your Web sites and the vicinities on the Web that matter
to your customers, as they are beacons of information and burgeoning
conversations. By doing this, you can be the first to uncover trends or
changes in the marketplace. You don't have to be on the outbound side
of marketing for this to be important. Creative thinking around product design, marketability, product naming, unique value, and so much
more is core to success.

And although it may be asking too much to know everything about
the universe, marketers should know everything *in* their universe. No
only how to implement the best possible programs, but deeply understand the product, competitors, and marketplace.

The Technology-Savvy Marketer

The best way to get to know technology is to use it. Smart marketers
are early adopters. There are many free demos, open-source software,
and exciting new electronics to try. *What sparks your interest? What
did the vendor do right to capture your attention and keep you involved?
What do you like about the product? Do you feel compelled to talk about
it?* Well, do that. Tell your friends, colleagues and family—become a
natural connector.

Do you use Firefox (or haven't you bothered to get off Internet Explorer)? Do you have a MySpace page? LinkedIn? Flickr? Do you blog? It will be much easier to guide implementations of wikis, blogs, podcasts, and RSS feeds in your company if you are a regular user of all of them. Not to mention, trying at least one new thing each week will propel your creative energy. Marketing is now a discipline steeped in technology, which requires marketers get comfortable with everything digital and build a deeper understanding of new and advanced technologies on the Web. You will have to participate in the social aspects of the Web to grasp community behaviors. You should comment on the blogs you visit, join social sites, set up an avatar, and try out a virtual world—seep yourself into the experience. It's easy to intellectualize all of this stuff, but the value is in experiencing.

You should be the first person to bring these new technologies in-house; start the first wiki, and show others how to be open and porous. There are vast opportunities that will be uncovered when you open the door for others to comment on or edit your ideas. A good place to start is with a wiki for each of the products your company ships, where a broader set of employees can add, edit, or comment. For the first time, sales reps will be able to see their input making a difference. No longer can one product manager be the gatekeeper for all information pertaining to a product. Now they are the managing editor, so more information and ideas will make it into the discussion.

Although putting the entire marketing and communications strategy and plan on a wiki may seem odd, it can be exponentially more valuable to plan in an open forum. It will likely become a cultural norm. While top-down management behaviors marginalize new and different ideas, peer communication empowers them, and peer interaction is what a wiki offers.

The Marketer's Dilemma

Every company needs to strike a balance between the two extremes of moving too slow or moving to fast. They need to determine how much research is required before making a decision. Ignoring all market planning, for example, is risky business, just as getting bogged down by excessive research annihilates innovation. Remaining insular will surely cause a company to struggle going forward. This research-or-run quagmire is the marketer's prime dilemma. It epitomizes the old way of thinking. *When does market and customer research enhance my product's chance of success, and when does it get in the way? How do I focus on customers and myriad marketing activities, yet spend enough time pondering customer value? Do I stick to enhancing current product or service capabilities, or should I jump to a new and better strategy?*

Although the problem is fundamental, companies and more specifically marketers that incorporate the Live Web into their process will more easily respond. Marketing has historically failed to manage the balance between knowledge, intuition, and execution. Too many marketing activities get off track and too many marketing people fail to see changes in the marketplace or in the competition. Using old processes confuses and slows execution. Inspiration must come from passion, experience, *and* learning across corporate boundaries and outside corporate walls. When this happens, companies gain the ability to make decisions quickly. Marketing leads, driving forward rather than looking back.

Speaking to the dilemma of getting a winning product to market without spending mind-boggling days, months, and possibly years researching, writing, and negotiating a product specification, Marissa Mayer, a Google vice president, has been widely quoted for saying that Google prefers throwing wet noodles at a wall to see which stick. Innovation and time-to-market are Google's driving force. Google's competitors have grown far beyond Yahoo!, MSN, and Ask.com to include such upstarts as Pronto, Snap, Powerset, Yandex, Baidu, Zoom-Info, Amazon, Technorati, and Alexa.[1] Each is working hard to slice up the search market by region, function, or category, and take a piece of the action. Google must continue to innovate to ensure its revenue growth rate (and therefore, its stock price), and they are doing it by ingraining innovation into the company culture, and leveraging the best known resource in high tech: people outside the company. Often, Google makes new products available for free on its well-traveled Web site prior to doing a thorough analysis of the market, competition, and alternatives. In this way, early users can check it out and provide the company with market feedback. Google illustrates one of the many ways to get to market fast. The company understands *Internet time.*

Not all companies understand how to move fast enough to keep up with the innovation, new companies, and cultural change driven by the Web. The meaning of fast has been lost on Coca-Cola, a company that has experienced a surprising slide over the past ten years. Long a marketing leader, Coke became entrenched in market research and planning. They stopped moving forward and taking risks.[2] The inspiration was gone. And in 2005, for the first time in the long-running competition between PepsiCo and Coca-Cola, Pepsi bested Coke with greater market capitalization. Pepsi had initiated many small businesses quickly, collaborating with partners, and finding success with several of them. The company's value has gone up significantly, while Coke has been stuck in the mud.

In Marketing 2.0, the fundamental discipline around how to make good decisions fast will be driven by real-time analysis and understanding of markets, customers, and competitors, a process unavailable to marketers just a few years ago. It's essential to have an abundance of knowledge but not get stuck in the research or run quandary.

Think Like an Underdog

Winners have nowhere to go but down. Arrogance and the trappings that come with winning cause myopia, and management loses sight of what's really happening with customers, and in the marketplace. When you're winning, it's difficult to embrace change. Companies that think like an underdog no matter how well they are doing are able to keep their edge, and continually re-think their products and approach to the marketplace. *How can you change the dynamics of the marketplace to put competitors (no matter how small) at a disadvantage?* Every feature, function, or service is up for grabs and open to new ideas or change, so the rules never stay the same. You have to keep raising the bar. The biggest challenge to staying ahead of the curve—and competitors—is having the courage to kill your own products, instead of waiting for someone else to do it for you. Wall Street condemns companies that introduce a product designed to cannibalize an older, successful product, but that's the best thing a company can do. It is important to innovate the little things, but don't be afraid to rethink the entire marketplace and replace your product with something much better. *You want to be the one to change the rules.*

Often marketers get mired down by the design and extend paradigm. Marketing and product development create a product definition, build the product, then add features as requested by customers or incorporated by competitors. When the product is feature rich and doesn't appear to require much attention, its resources are diverted to other projects. That's what we call a cash cow. *If you stop investing in a product, how do customers respond?* They get frustrated and go somewhere else. If they are locked into buying your product, they develop a negative image of the company, and eventually another company will come along and reinvent the space. *Cash cows are bad for business.*[3] Divest or reinvest. Even a tired product bringing in single-digit profits can find inspiration from a dedicated customer base. Marketers must constantly strive for new perspective (on an old product), and track how customer values have changed.

Today, it is better to share information with a broader group internally, and share appropriate information externally. Marketers can work to eliminate silo and insular behaviors common in most companies. Silos, where employees protect their territory, minimize the innovative and interactive activities that create success. And the insular behaviors often extend to interactions with audiences outside the company. *Can you post your corporate presentations online?*[4] *Can you determine which confidential information impacts revenue and competi-*

tiveness, and which information doesn't really need to be kept private?
Allow your audiences to learn more about what your company is doing
and where you are headed. Let them share that information with others. Determine which slides and documents would be better off shared,
linked to, and re-used.

Much of our success going forward will be based on the ability to
plan and implement with speed and accuracy. The luxury of time for
long drawn out research projects and sixty-page product specifications
is gone. Marketing 2.0 in the age of engage will be based on the ability
to think fast on your feet, be open to the thoughts and ideas of others,
and the willingness to take calculated risks. Marketing's reinvention
has been driven by the thousands of public voices marketers must contend with, where competing words aren't just from competitors and
the press, but are from customers, interested parties, partners, and employees. Our power to influence will be based on how well we monitor and manage these communications. Now that the information we
need is available in real-time, and we have access to the minds and
clicks of millions of people, anything is possible.

9 | Throw Out Your Marketing Plan

IN THE AGE OF ENGAGE COMPANIES MUST BE OPEN,
AUTHENTIC, AND INTERACTIVE.

An open company will enable and encourage their audiences to become involved with the company and their brands. They will share revenue, collaborate with partners, and act on innovative ideas no matter where they are generated. An authentic company has a vision for the market and their customers and a passion for creating change. The company voice is clear and strong. And a company that defines and designs its marketing around audience interactions will gain greater customer and market knowledge and attract larger and more loyal audiences. Open, authentic, and interactive—these are the qualities of companies that will win in the age of engage.

Real-Time Planning

The first step is to change the way you build a strategy and plan. Writing a sixty-page product specification or twenty-page analysis of the potential for a buzz campaign is limited in value. These documents are often built by a single person or a small team with little outside input, and they will simply gather dust. What's needed is a living document. Using Live Web technology internally to create an open, social, and interactive environment will take marketing to new heights. Every product plan, marketing strategy, marketing communications or marketing program document should be implemented via a wiki. Put it online and make it open to a broad set of internal resources to review, edit, and comment.

A marketing plan wiki should be incorporated into an internal Web page that includes live feeds from competitor blogs, industry blogs, key press, and any other useful real-time information. The marketing plan wiki is marketing-central for the company—the page everyone logs onto first thing in the morning to know the strategy, plan, activities, and outcomes.[1]

It isn't possible to visualize an interactive Web site through the flat interface of a book. So instead, I invite you to visit www.MarketingReinvented.com to see an example of the new way to create a marketing strategy and plan.

Continue
the Conversation

www.AgeofEngage.com

Interviews, examples, and cool companies blog plus
free resources and essential Web site links

www.MarketingReinvented.com

The Marketing Plan Wiki

Marketing Exercises

Following is a list of questions, organized by chapter, to help you think through your strategy. This is a good place to start as you begin the process to reinvent your marketing and your company.

1. Made to Engage

1. What age of engage stage are you in?
   - Learning/researching
   - Planning
   - Executing
   - Innovating

2. If you haven't gotten started, what is holding you back?

3. Define your interactions with customers. Do you interact with them at a deep enough level to find creative solutions to their problems? Do you reward them for providing input?

4. How can customers help create your product? Could you collaborate in real-time via wiki?

5. Do you invite customers to provide stories or tutorials in their own words, and post them on your Web site?

6. In what ways is your company open to input from outsiders on products, technologies, innovations, or marketing?

2. Think Venture

1. What business are you in? How can you broaden the definition? What are you doing to change your industry?

2. What does your market look like (competitors, target audience)? Which companies stand out and for what reasons? What isn't being done well for customers or a segment of customers?

3. What philosophies drive your company and guide your employees?

4. How can you make your company or department more porous and open to outside ideas and influences?

5. How do you encourage out-of-the-box thinking and behavior (and minimize not-invented-here, we-don't-do-it-that-way thinking)?

6. What do you offer for free to customers and prospects to entice them to learn more, and to trust you as an authority in your market?

7. How can you change the rules in your marketplace? Is it possible to offer the core product for free and charge for services or supporting added value?

8. How can you organize your company so that an integrated, innovative, whole product solution comes out every time, and so that other employees feel comfortable commenting on the product or catching errors before the product hits the market?

9. How can you encourage, support, and compensate employees in a way that they will put creating extraordinary products above their personal objectives?

10. Where can you start implementing wikis? Who should be invited to collaborate with the core team or people?

11. How can you open up key subjects to internal debate, and encourage outsider thinking, provocative insights, and criticism?

12. Write a list of what is proprietary information and what can be shared openly on your Web site, on partner Web sites, or on SlideShare.net.

3. Value Reborn

1. What does your organization do well, and what are the reasons why you do it so well?

2. What are the dominant technical skills (core competencies) of the product development group?

3. What are the key process skills in your organization?

4. Which competency helps the company stand out from the competition the most?

5. How does the competency translate into the product or service?

6. How is the competency/value unique? Will competitors easily provide the same solution?

7. How can the competency or unique capability be defended and sustained (enhanced and strengthened) over time?

8. How can the company apply the competency in unique ways to create unique value, or target unique opportunities?

9. Does the product, value, or uniqueness create a new segment or category in the marketplace?

10. How does the product (and unique value) engage and delight customers?

11. How can you provide an inherent feature or function in the product (or Web site) that makes customers continually interact with it or want to come back for more?

12. How can you solve a customer problem in a completely new way?

13. How can you continually add value or reinvent value in the product? Are there areas of differentiation outside of the product? Is there a unique competency in sales, service, or financing processes?

14. Is there a soft need (emotion or desire) met by the product that can be exploited?

15. How does the unique value affect the price of the product?

16. What methods or processes can you use to drive the unique value across the company and into every employee?

17. Will people want to talk about this product because it is interesting, exciting, and/or meeting an unmet need or want? What methods will you use to get them talking?

4. Voice

1. What is your company passionate about?

2. What is the vision? What is the company point-of-view in terms of the product, the market, and the world?

3. Where is the industry going? Where is the company taking customers?

4. What trends point to the direction the company is going?

5. What tone, style, or personality does the company express?

6. How have you made the message believable? What proof points can you use?

7. How can you reposition your competition and put them in a box (show their strategy as narrow)?

8. How can you define or redefine the marketplace to show that you offer the unique value most coveted?

9. How can you open up a dialogue with customers? Do you have a blog or social interactions on your Web site? Is there regular many-to-many conversations taking place?

10. Do you blog? Do you encourage everyone around you to blog? How can your blog affect change with your target audience?

5. Verifiable

1. Is your company credible? Are you positioned as an authority in your industry? If not, who is the authority and how can you take that position away or partner with them?

2. Is your company authentic? How do you ensure there are consistent, believable behaviors across the company that support the company style, positioning, and communications?

3. How do you ensure customers are treated with respect at every touchpoint?

4. How do you make sure the company delivers on all of its commitments?

5. What methods do you use to create deep, long-term relationships with partners, press, and bloggers?

6. How are you approaching and interacting with early adopters and advocates? How can you make them an integrated part of your company and share with them?

7. What tools, techniques, and behaviors do you employ to persuade your audience to believe your message and voice?

6. Know Your Vicinity

1. How well do you know your target audience? What Web sites, social networks, Web TV sites, and virtual worlds do they visit?

2. Have you deployed behavioral targeting? What are you learning about your customers, and how are you incorporating that information into your product, Web site, and messaging?

3. How can you impact third-party ratings sites? Can you give points or prizes to your brand advocates for writing positive comments?

4. How can you get involved in social networking? Does your company have a page on MySpace? Have you developed a widget for Facebook?

5. How can you build community by creating a wiki or social network for you market (without it being too self-serving)?

6. How can you embrace resellers and affiliates to extend your brand and positioning? Can you share reputation or revenue? What methods, tools, or processes can you deploy to integrate them deeply into your company, and interact with them more often?

7. Drive the Vehicle

1. How can you organize so that all marketing activities support the strategic value, and so that all programs have a digital element that is consistent and cohesive?

2. What are you doing to ensure your message is consistent across all venues and marketing programs (digital and traditional)?

3. How are you monitoring all of the vicinities on the Web where your customers and prospects congregate? How are you participating in the conversation?

4. What social elements have you added to your corporate Web site? How can customers congregate and interact there?

5. How can you encourage customers to submit personal experiences with your product or company (through audio tutorials or videos)?

6. How can you add video that entertains while educating rather than forcing consumers to read through several pages of materials?

7. Are you measuring your marketing activities? Do they deliver on the core message? Did they reach credible and influential sources? What elements of the product or service showed the most traction?

8. How can you try out viral, word-of-mouth, and virtual worlds on a small scale? In what creative ways and venues can you reach your target audience?

9. What is your plan for interacting with people who play with your brand in ways you are not comfortable?

10. How can you turn unplanned user behavior into value-add?

8. Sitting on a Rocket

1. What tools can you deploy to help make decisions quickly? Is your company diverse enough that you could deploy a decision market?

2. How are you using wikis and RSS to keep yourself and your employees informed? How can you enhance or extend this work?

3. How is your company or marketing department embracing and incorporating new Web technology, features, or functions?

4. How can you stop long, drawn-out processes that create slow product iterations, and get to market quickly?

5. In what ways do you ensure employees are always looking for an edge, a way to stay ahead of the competition?

9. Throw Out Your Marketing Plan

1. Have you put your marketing strategy and plan on a wiki?

NOTES

1. Made to Engage

1. The term "Web 2.0" was coined by O'Reilly vice president Dale Dougherty in 2004, although credit is often given to Tim O'Reilly. Tim O'Reilly, "What is Web 2.0?" www.oreillynet.com (September 30, 2005) http://www.oreillynet.com/pub/a/oreilly/tim/news/2005/09/30/what-is-web-20.html.

2. John Markoff, a writer for *The New York Times*, is commonly given credit for coining the term "Web 3.0." John Markoff, "Entrepreneurs See a Web Guided by Common Sense," *The New York Times*, (November 12, 2006) http://www.nytimes.com/2006/11/12business/12web.html?ex=1183953600&en=8dab68ab6372a7bf&ei=5070.

3. Doc Searls, "Linux for Suits — The World Live Web," *Linux Journal* (October 31, 2005) http://interactive.linuxjournal.com/article/8549.

4. Shira Ovide, "Weak Ad Sales Weigh on Newspapers," *The Wall Street Journal*, (April 19, 2007).

5. Sarah Ellison, "Circulation Falls at Many Papers," *The Wall Street Journal*, (May 1, 2007) http://online.wsj .com/article/SB117794322255886957-search.html?KEYWORDS=circulation+falls+at+many+papers&COL LECTION=wsjie/6month.

6. Jon Fine, "London's New Media Lessons," *BusinessWeek*, (December 4, 2006).

7. Josee Rose and Rob Fisher, "McClatchy Posts $279 Million Loss," *The Wall Street Journal*, (February 6, 2007) http://online.wsj.com/article_print/SB117077185078099559.html.

8. Wendy Davis, "Citizen Journalists Rush Online," MediaPost, (October 12, 2006) http://blogs.medipost.c om/online_minute/?p=1356.

9. Marshall Kirkpatrick, "YouTube Serves 100M Videos Each Day," TechCrunch, (July 17, 2006) http:/www. techcrunch.com/2006/07/17/youtube-serves-100m-videos-each-day/.

10. Mark Zuckerberg, CEO of Facebook stated at the F8 Facebook Developers Conference, May 24, 2007, that Facebook is growing by 100,000 new visitors each month, and more than 60 percent of users are outside of college. "Teens, Adults Spur 89 percent Facebook Visitor Increase," MarketingVox (July 9, 2007) http://www.marketingvox.com/archives/2007/07/09/teens-adults-spur-89-percent-facebook-visitor-increase/.

11. The term Marketing 2.0 appeared in the *The Wall Street Journal* in an article by Robert A. Guth, "How Microsoft is Learning to Love Online Advertising," (November 16, 2006), but the term started appearing about six months earlier. Karl Long at MarketingProfs Daily Fix commented on the "2.0" hyperbole being applied to the Web, advertising, agencies, etc. in his article, "Marketing 2.0: What's in a Name?" (June 5, 2006).

12. You can find the JetBlue Airways and CEO David Neeleman apology video here: http://www.youtube .com/watch?v=-r_PIg7EAUw.

13. Dawn Kawamoto and Elinor Mills, "AOL Apologizes for Release of User Search Data," CNET (August 7, 2006) http://news.com.com/2100-1030_3-6102793.html.

14. Tom Siebert, "McFlog? McDonald's Proves Wal-Mart Has No Monopoly On Fake Blogs," MediaPost (November 6, 2006) http://publications.mediapost.com/index.cfm?fuseaction=Articles.showArticle&art_aid=50669.

15. Find Doc Searls' entire essay on the Live Web, which appeared in the *Linux Journal*, at http://interactive.linuxjournal.com/article/8549.

16. Don Tapscott and Anthony D. Williams, "The Wiki Workplace," *Business Week* (March 26, 2007) http://www.businessweek.com/innovate/content/mar2007/id20070326_237620.htm?chan=search.

17. Find out more about Nova Spivack at http://novaspivack.typepad.com/, and read more about Web 3.0 in Nova Spivak's article, "The Third-Generation Web is Coming," KurzweilAI.net (December 17, 2006) http://www.kurzweilai.net/articles/art0689.html.

18. Louise Story, "New Bar Codes Can Talk with Your Cellphone," *The New York Times* (April 1, 2007).

2. Think Venture

1. Paula Lehman, "Free Downloads—After This Message," *Business Week*, (October 9, 2006).

2. "Big Pharma's Nurse Will See You Now," *Business Week* (June 12, 2006)

3. Denise Shiffman worked at Sun Microsystems from 1991–2001. One of her management roles was as Vice President of Marketing for the Storage Systems Group where she interfaced with the service organization.

4. W.L. Gore & Associates regularly receives accolades for their unique approach to management and organizational behavior. More information about the dynamic of their corporate culture can be found on their Web site, http://www.gore.com/en_xx/aboutus/culture/index.html.

5. Alvin Toffler first coined the term "prosumer" in his book *The Third Wave* (New York: Bantam Books, 1980)

6. Don Tapscott and Anthony D. Williams, "Peer Innovation and Production," *BusinessWeek* (February 12, 2007) http://www.businessweek.com/innovate/content/feb2007/id20070212_914411.htm?chan=search

7. For more on iPod hacks, http://ipodlinux.org/, http://www.ipodhacks.com/.

8. Louise Story, "An Upstart Challenges Google," *The New York Times* (February 26, 2007).

9. Martin Fackler, "Inside Japan's Puzzle Palace," *The New York Times* (March 21, 2007).

10. Sarah Lacy and Jessi Hempel, "Valley Boys," *BusinessWeek* (August 14, 2006) http://www.business week .com/magazine/content/06_33/b3997001.htm.

11. Number of Digg monthly users as of this writing. Jason Pontin, "A Social-Networking Service with a Velvet Rope," *The New York Times* (July 29, 2007).

12. Andrew Martin, "Does Coke Need A Refill?" *The New York Times* (May 27, 2007).

13. "HP Enters Home Digital Photo Market," *Newsbytes* (now part of *The Washington Post*) (March 17, 1997).

14. Robert D. Hof, "The Power of Us," *BusinessWeek* (June 20, 2005) http://www.businessweek.com/magazine/content/05_25/b3938601.htm?chan=search.

15. John Markoff, "Entrepreneurs See A Web Guided By Common Sense," *The New York Times*, (November 12, 2006).

3. Value Reborn

1. David Haskin "What Microsoft Must Do to Make Zune a Success," *PC World, Computerworld* (March 31, 2007) http://www.pcworld.com/article/id,130283-c,mp3players/article.html.

2. Roger O. Crockett, "Honing the Razr Edge," *BusinessWeek*, (May 28, 2007).

3. Roger O. Crockett, "Motorola Sharpens the Razr Edge," *BusinessWeek*, (January 20, 2005).

4. David Pogue, "Paying More for a Printer, But Less for Ink" *The New York Times* (May 17, 2007) http://www.nytimes.com/2007/05/17/technology/17pogue.html?ex=1337054400&en=0d0fc2e6a84ceb30&ei=5090.

5. Steve Lohr, "I.B.M. Showing that Giants Can Be Nimble," *The New York Times* (July 18, 2007) http://www.nytimes.com/2007/07/18/technology/18blue.html?ei=5070&en=60532345083a1031&ex=1185595200&adxnnl=1&adxnnlx=1185486814-QbQnEs3k6i3Y6NZ5gycsA.

6. Pete Engardio, "Toyota: How the Hybrid Race Went to the Swift," *BusinessWeek*, (January 29, 2007) http://www.businessweek.com/magazine/content/07_05/b4019006.htm?chan=search.

7. Ethan Smith and Kevin J. Delaney, "Music Companies Pull Videos from Fuse Network and Yahoo," *The Wall Street Journal* (September 28, 2006). An aditional source was Wikipedia, http://en.wikipedia.org/wiki /Music_video.

8. Jessi Hempel, "Craigslist's Ongoing Success Story," *BusinessWeek* (May 15, 2007) http://www.businessweek.com/innovate/content/may2007/id20070515_301894.htm?chan=search.

9. John Battelle, *The Search* (New York: Penguin Group, 2005).

10. Google is a great example of branding through marketability built into the product. AdSense ads appear with the Google name. Customers continually go to the Google branded site to perform their search. And every company Web site or blog that incorporates the Google search function puts the brand on their home page, and all of their Web pages for that matter.

11. Jeffrey S. Young and William L. Simon, *Icon: The Greatest Second Act in the History of Business* (New Jersey: John Wiley & Sons, Inc., 2005).

12. There is much debate on the subject of whether digital music downloads are helping the industry or hurting it. Apple states the music industry earned one billion dollars from digital downloads with no added cost, Jeff Leeds, "EMI to Drop Digital Locks in Web Sales," *The New York Times* (April 3, 2007). In their article, "Online Customers Are Good for the Music Business," (January 5, 2007), eMarketer reported on numbers from Nielson SoundScan and the Digital Media Association indicating that online customers are revitalizing the music industry. However, according to others, CD sales are decelerating faster than digital downloads are increasing to make up for the gap which is hurting the music industry, Ethan Smith, "Sales of Music, Long in Decline, Plunge Sharply," *The Wall Street Journal* (March 21, 2007).

13. Source: Espressotec, http://www.espressotec.com/history.asp, Wikipedia, http://en.wikipedia.org/wiki/Starbucks.

14. Burt Helm, "Saving Starbucks' Soul," *BusinessWeek* (April 9, 2007) http://www.businessweek.com/magaz ine/content/07_15/b4029070.htm?chan=search.

15. Joseph A. Michelli, *The Starbucks Experience* (New York: McGraw-Hill Books, 2007).

4. Voice

1. Theodore Levitt's *Harvard Business Review* article titled "Marketing Myopia" can be purchased at http://harvardbusinessonline.hbsp.harvard.edu/b02/en/com mon/item_detail.jhtml?id=R0407L&referral=2340.

2. Find a bit more background on the evolution of the Blendtec videos in this article, Laura Lorber, "Marketing Videos Became a Hit in Their Own Right," *The Wall Street Journal* (July 2, 2007) http://online.wsj.com/public/article/SB118330775119654449.html.html?mod=sblink_feature_articles.

3. Bobby White, "Firms Take a Cue From YouTube," *The Wall Street Journal* (January 2, 2007).

4. To see pictures from the Adidas Adicolor campaign, go to http://experience themessage.typepad.com/blog/2006 /05/adidas_gets_the.html.

5. Eric Pfanner, "Hewlett-Packard Takes a New Tack: Being Cool," *The New York Times* (July 25, 2006) http://www.nytimes.com/2006/07/25/business/media/25adco.html?ex=1185681600&en=bcfba52027a90734&ei=5070.

6. Yvon Chouinard, *Let My People Go Surfing* (New York: Penguin Books, 2005).

7. Sources: "Product Life Story Labels," Springwise.com (June 5, 2007) http://www.springwise.com/food_beve rage/product_life_story_labels/, and DoleOrganic.com

8. The anti-EMC strategy was spearheaded by Janpieter Scheerder, Shiffman, Bill Cook, and Ron Lloyd.

9. Burt Helm, "Saving Starbucks' Soul," *BusinessWeek* (April 9, 2007) http://www.businessweek.com/magaz ine/content/07_15/b4029070.htm?chan=search.

10. Shiffman led the media-server organization at Sun Microsystems in the mid-1990s.

11. There were several deals in 2007 including Viacom's agreement to provide content through the Web TV site Joost and *The New York Times* Company's collaboration with Monster Worldwide and their Monster.com jobs-listing site. There was also the announcement of a collaboration between News Corp and NBC to challenge YouTube; Richard Sikols, "News Corp. and NBC in Web Deal," *The New York Times* (March 23, 2007) http://www.nytimes.com/2007/03/23/technology/23video.html?ei=5070&en=901ced828545070e&ex=1186113600&adxnnl=1&adxnnlx=1186002817-hj1Oscni4+BtlCOxdeXG+Q.

12. In 2006, Disney's ABC TV network led the charge offering popular TV programs on ABC.com for free the night after the program airs. They also offer TV programs for a fee on iTunes. CBS has partnered with everyone from Amazon, Apple, and Yahoo to Bebo, Brightcove, Netvibes, and Veoh to distribute content. NBC Universal distributes content online through widgets, giving users the capability to post NBC programming on their blogs, personal profiles, or Web sites.

13. Hugh MacLeod, "Blogging Doubled Stormhoek Sales in Less Than Twelve Months," Gapingvoid (December 29, 2005) http://www.gapingvoid.com/ Moveable_Type/archives/002112.html. MacLeod updated the numbers a year later to a five-fold revenue increase in two years in this post http://www.gap ingvoid.com/Moveable_Type/archives/003577.html.

14. Get more information on which Fortune 1000 companies are blogging here at http://www.socialtext.net/bizblogs/index.cgi and at http://www.thenewpr.com/ wiki/pmwiki.php?pagename=Resources.CorporateBlogsList.

15. Tech-savvy companies know to set the rules for how employees or outside users should interact on their Web entities. A public discourse policy can be a few words on the Web site or blog home page or can be a more-detailed document such as this one used by Sun Microsystems targeted to employees, http://www.sun.com/aboutsun/media/blogs/policy.html.

5. Verifiable

1. Daniel Gilbert, "Compassionate Commercialism," *The New York Times* (March 25, 2007).

2. Shankar Gupta, "Sony Shutters PSP Flog," MediaPost's Online Media Daily (December 18, 2006) http://publications.mediapost.com/index.cfm?fuse action=Articles.showArticle&art_aid=52679.

3. Walter J. Carl, Ph.D., "To Tell or Not to Tell? Assessing the Practical Effects of Disclosure for World-of-Mouth Marketing Agents and Their Conversational Partners," Northeastern University (2006) http://www.waltercarl.neu.edu/ downloads.

4. In 2007, Google appeared on the Interbrand Top 100 Brands at number twenty. Although Coca-Cola still ranks number one (Pepsi is number twenty six), as computers and Internet connections reach third-world countries in volume, Google's brand rating will most likely increase organically. Google has an automatic advantage every time someone new connects to the Internet. Where Coke has to spend ad dollars to gain a similar advantage. David Kiley, "Best Global Brands: How the BusinessWeek/Interbrand Top 100 Companies are Using Their Brands to Fuel Expansion," *BusinessWeek* (August 7, 2006).

5. Personal politics aside, this is a good story illustrating how confusion diminishes the message, and how confusion can be a tactic to weaken your competitors. Sources: EnvironmentalDefense.org, James Wolcott, "Rush to Judgment," *Vanity Fair* (May 2007), and Robert F. Kennedy, Jr., "Texas Chainsaw Management," *Vanity Fair* (May 2007).

6. Know Your Vicinity

1. Robert D. Hof, "It's a Whole New Web, and This Time Around it will be Built By You," *BusinessWeek* (September 26, 2005).

2. Coke's negative and out-of-touch response to the highly entertaining video went viral across the Web. Spokesperson Susan McDermott had said, "We would hope people want to drink [Diet Coke] more than try experiments with it." Even though Diet Coke sales had been flat the previous year, the company didn't acknowledge the visibility the viral video gave them. She went on to say the "craziness with Mentos . . . doesn't fit with the brand personality" of Diet Coke. Suzanne Vranica and Chad Terhune, "Mixing Coke and Mentos Makes a Gusher of Publicity," *The Wall Street Journal* (June 12, 2006) http://online.wsj.com/public/article/SB115007602216777497-1mzdx_pOFlMBwo9UAiqbsgY 6MZ0_20060619.ht ml?mod=blogs.

3. Lev Grossman, "Invention of the Year," *Time* (November 2006) http://www.time.com/time/2006/tech guide best inventions/inventions/youtube2.html.

4. Jamin Warren and John Jurgensen, "The Wizards of Buzz," *The Wall Street Journal* (February 10, 2007) http://online.wsj.com/public/article/SB117106531769704150-zpK10wf4CJOB4IKoJS5anuNoi6Y_20080209.html.

5. Source: ComScore Media Metrix, http://www.comscore.com/press/releaseasp?press=1019.

6. Source: Entertainment Software Association, "Essential Facts About the Computer and Video Game Industry," (2007) http://www.theesa.com/archives/ESA-F%202007%20F.pdf.

7. Bill McMahon, "Viral Music Sales Through Widgets," Springwise (June 24, 2007) http://www.springwise.com/media_publishing/viral_music_sales_through_widg/.

8. Miguel Helft, "Contributors on YouTube May Share Advertising Revenue," *The New York Times* (May 5, 2007) http://www.nytimes.com/2007/05/05/technology/05tube.html?ex=1186113600&en=9459f63a49e15460&ei=5070.

9. Trendwatching defines enterprising consumers who use their favorite Web sites to earn extra cash as *minipreneurs*. They are part of a generation Trendwatching calls Generation C(ash), and companies are offering revenue sharing, reward schemes, and gifts to attract these consumers, http://www.trend watching.com/trends/gen-cash.htm

10. The power of advocates is being measured. In a study by Yahoo, it was found that an influential, vocal advocate talking up your product could generate three times more product revenue than a less vocal peer. Rebecca Lieb, "How Do You Influence the Influencers?" ClickZ Experts (June 1, 2007) http://www.clickz.com/showPage.html?page=3626006.

7. Drive the Vehicle

1. Kristen Philipkoski, "Furniture Causes FedEx Fits," *Wired* (August 11, 2005) http://www.wired.com/culture /lifestyle/news/2005/08/68492.

2. Miguel Helft and Geraldine Fabrikant, "WhoseTube? Viacom Sues Google Over Video Clips," *The New York Times* (March 14, 2007) http://www.nytimes.com/2007/03/14/technology/14viacom.html?ex=1186113600&en=0c3177cb611 38f2b&ei=5070.

3. Louise Lee, "Catalogs, Catalogs, Everywhere," *BusinessWeek* (December 4, 2006) http://www.businessweek.com/magazine/content/06_49/b4012049.htm?chan =search.

4. Aili McConnon, "The Mind-Bending New World of Work," *BusinessWeek* (April 2, 2007) http://www.businessweek.com/magazine/content/07_14/b4028001. htm.

5. Here are the relevant Engadget articles, http://www.engadget.com/2004/09/14/kryptonite-evolution-2000-u-lock-hacked-by-a-bic-pen/, http://www.engad get.com/2004/09/16/hacking-the-evolution-2000-bike-lock-with-a-bic-pen-kryptonite/, http://www.engadget.com/2004/09/19/kryptonite-offers-free-up grades-for-easily-picke-bike-locks/.

6. "Adidas' World Cup Shutout," *BusinessWeek* (April 3, 2006) http://www.busi nessweek.com/magazine/content/06_14/b3978079.htm?chan=search.

7. "How IBM Used Live Webcams Plus Chat to Impress Mid-Market Prospects with Concierge-Style Marketing," *Marketing Sherpa* (January 19, 2007).

8. Larry Huston and Nabil Sakkab, "P&G's New Innovation Model," Harvard Business School Working Knowledge (March 20, 2006) http://hbswk.hbs.edu/ archive/5258. html.

9. Doritos marketing director Jason McDonnell spoke at the OMMA Conference and Expo Hollywood in March 2007.

10. Mae Anderson, "Dissecting 'Subservient Chicken,'" *Adweek* (March 7, 2005).

11. Additional reading on word of mouth, Evan Gerber, "Measure Word-of-Mouth Buzz," iMedia Connection (September 13, 2006) http://www.imediaconnec tion.com/content/11165.asp.

12. Source: Snopes.com, http://www.snopes.com/photos/advertisements/honda cog.asp.

13. Suzanne Vranica, "Laughing All the Way to the Bank," *The Wall Street Journal* (July 10, 2006) http://online.wsj.com/public/article/SB115221646616899861q_ m0RKzSAALmWoAv_x7a0cCo9EI_20060809.html.

14. Kerry Capell, "Wal-Mart with Wings," *BusinessWeek* (November 27, 2006) http://www.businessweek.com/globalbiz/content/nov2006/gb20061116_ 574456.htm?chan=search.

15. Brian Morrissey, "JC Penney Goes Beyond E-Mail with Desktop App," *Adweek* (June 15, 2007) http://www.adweek.com/aw/search/article_display.jsp?vnu_content_id=1003599526.

16. Reuters, "NBC to Let Other Web Site Post NBC Video," *PC Magazine* (June 6, 2007) www.pcmag.com/article2/0,1895,2142245,00.asp.

17. Kate Kaye, "Widgets are Trackable, but Ad Implications Unclear," ClickZ, (June 13, 2007) http://www.clickz.com/showPage.html?page=3626141.

18. David Bauder, The Associated Press, "TV Networks Thinking of Creative Ways to Keep You from Skipping Ads," *The Seattle Times* (May 29, 2007) http://archives.se attletimes.nwsource.com/cgi-in/texis.cgi/web/vortex/display?slug=webtvads2 9&date=20070529&query=tv+networks+thinking+of+creative+ways+to.

19. Jessica E. Vascellaro, "Online Retailers are Watching You," *The Wall Street Journal* (November 28, 2006) http://online.wsj.com/article/SB116467931445434072. html?mod=djemPJ.

20. Aaron O. Patrick, "Microsoft Ad Push is all About You," *The Wall Street Journal* (December 26, 2006) http://online.wsj.com/article_email/SB116709 123304359226-lMyQjAxMDE2NjI3NjAyOTYxWj.html.

21. Robert D. Hof, "The Power of Us," *BusinessWeek* (June 20, 2005).

8. Sitting on a Rocket

1. Charles S. Knight, "Top 100 Alternative Search Engines, February 2007," Read/ WriteWeb (February 27, 2007) http://www.readwriteweb.com/archives/top_ 100_alternative_search_engines_feb07.php.

2. Andrew Martin, "Does Coke Need A Refill?" *The New York Times* (May 27, 2007).

3. One of the best examples of a cash-cow product is Microsoft Office. The tools that make up Office are feature rich and require little change. They are the dominant leaders in their categories and they do not interoperate well with competitive products. Microsoft has known for almost ten years that software as a service over the Internet will eventually become the predominant solution, but it minimizes their ability to lock-in customers, and forces them to compete in a new market where they aren't a monopoly. In 2006 and 2007, there has been a real shift towards all types of applications that automatically connect to a hosting service or run on the hosting service—from business desktop applications to spam detection to customer resource management (CRM). Microsoft often comes to market late, slowly rolls out features, and controls the market they dominate. So far, that strategy hasn't worked for Zune, their media player, since they had no market position to begin with. They will need to shift gears to compete in new markets that have new rules. Kevin Delaney and Robert A. Guth, "Google's Free Web Services Will Vie with Microsoft

Office," *The Wall Street Journal* (October 11, 2006) http://online.wsj.com/ar
ticle/SB116052883714688829.html?mod=todays_us_marketplace.

4. Slidshare.net and YouTube are both good opportunities to share your company's
point of view. You can upload an internal, employee-made video that parodies a
competitor or yourselves, or you can upload a dynamic customer presentation
that gets a broader audience to understand your plan and company positioning.
Whether or not they become viral, they will enhance your communications.
You can point customers, prospects, partners, resellers, shareholders, and just
about anyone in your ecosystem to the content for easy access, and they can
pass it on.

9. Throw Out Your Marketing Plan

1. The Marketing Plan Wiki at MarketingReinvented.com is hosted by Wetpaint. I
chose Wetpaint because of their easy-to-use templates that give the pages a nice
visual element. The company used for the marketing plan example is Amanda's
Restaurants and is owned and run by my good friend Amanda West.

ABOUT THE AUTHOR

Denise Shiffman is founder and principal of the strategic marketing and innovation consultancy Venture Essentials. In her twenty-three-year marketing and management career, she has launched over thirty products responsible for over $2 billion in revenue, marketed pioneering computer and Web technologies, and reinvented the corporate brand of a Fortune 500 company. She voices her dynamic and market-changing perspective on her blog at www.ageofengage.com/blog. Her commentary has been featured in *The New York Times, BusinessWeek,* and CNET.

You can reach her by email at denise@ageofengage.com.

Contact Information:

Bulk orders and discounts
info@huntstreetpress.com

Book speaking engagements
speeches@ageofengage.com

Author's seminars
www.ageofengage.com/seminars

Publicity
denise@ageofengage.com

INDEX